Animal Mandala Adult Coloring Book Vol 2

60 Entertaining Stress Relieving Animal Patterns

By Omar Johnson

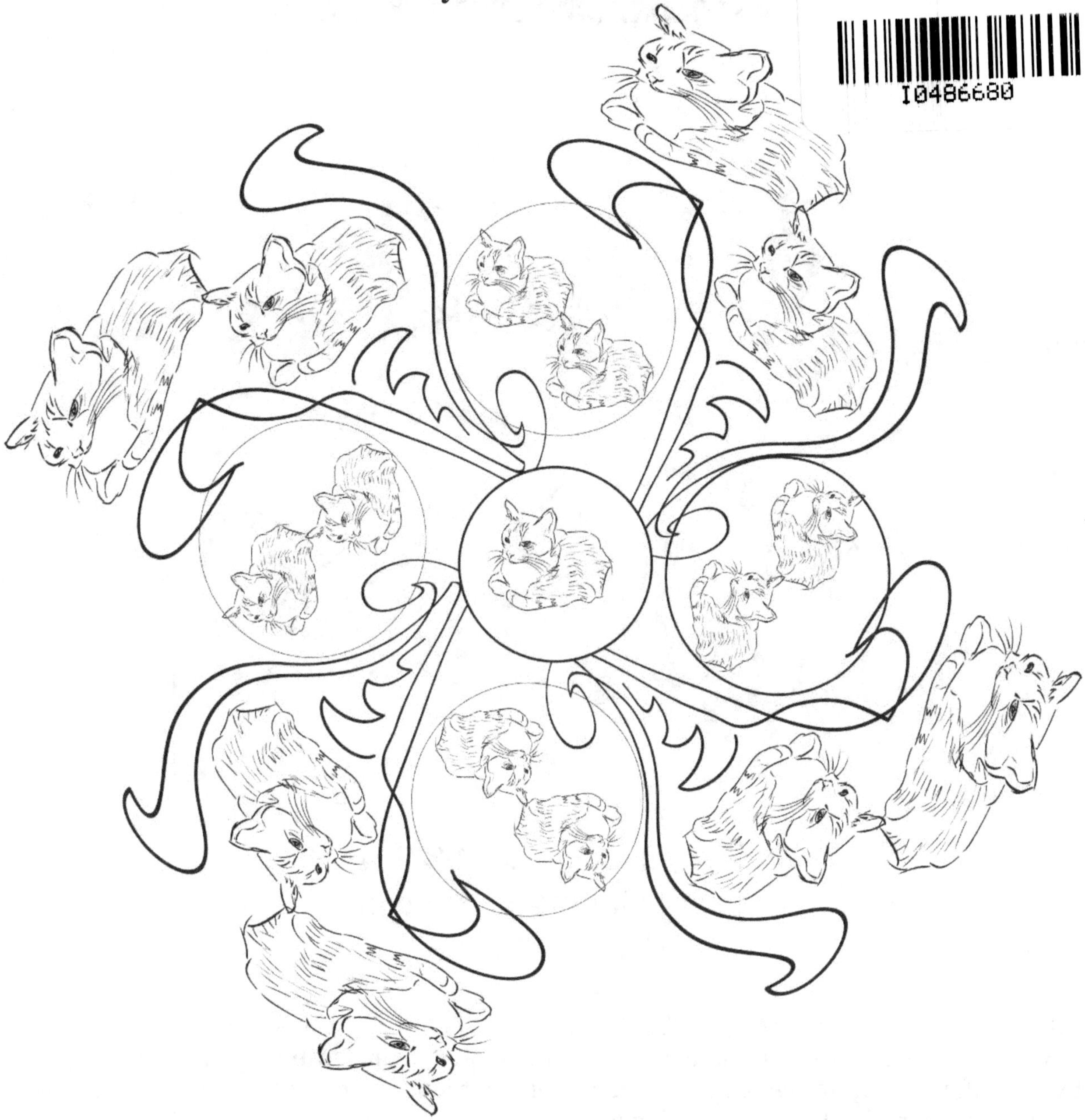

Get Your Free Mandala

Visit

ADULTCOLORINGBOOKSFORYOU.COM

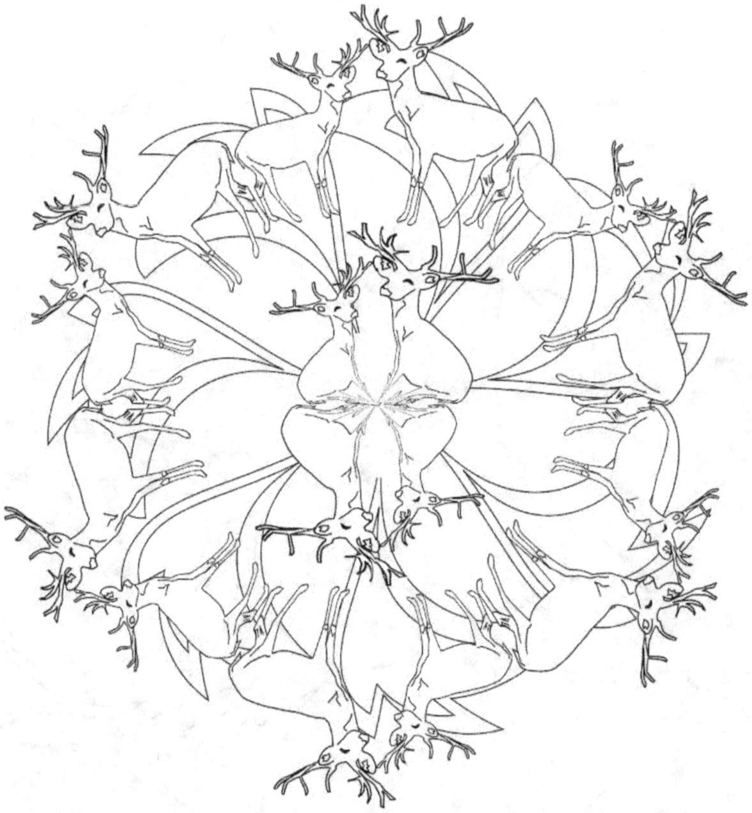

Make Profits Easy LLC Publishing
profitsdaily123@aol.com

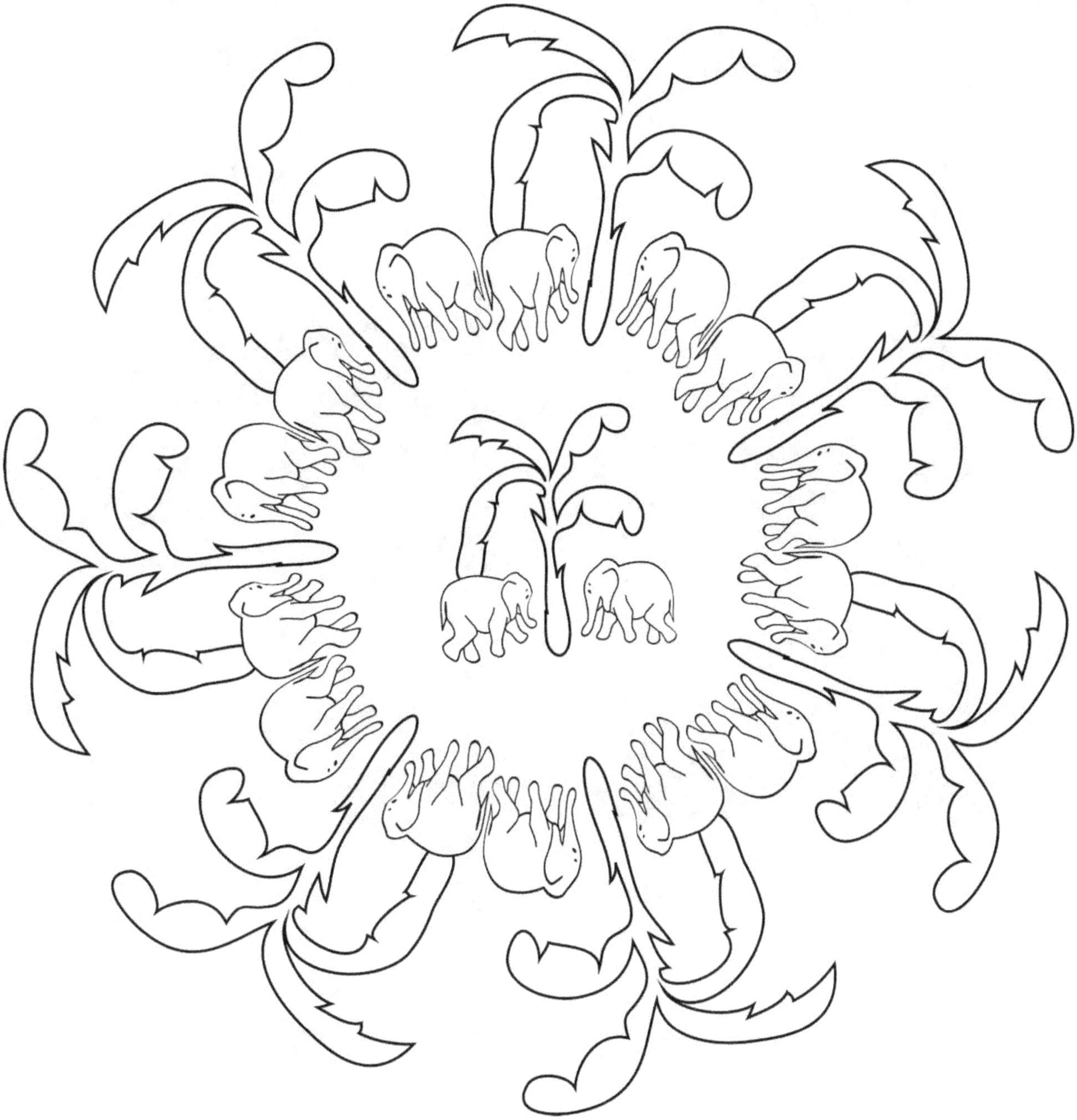

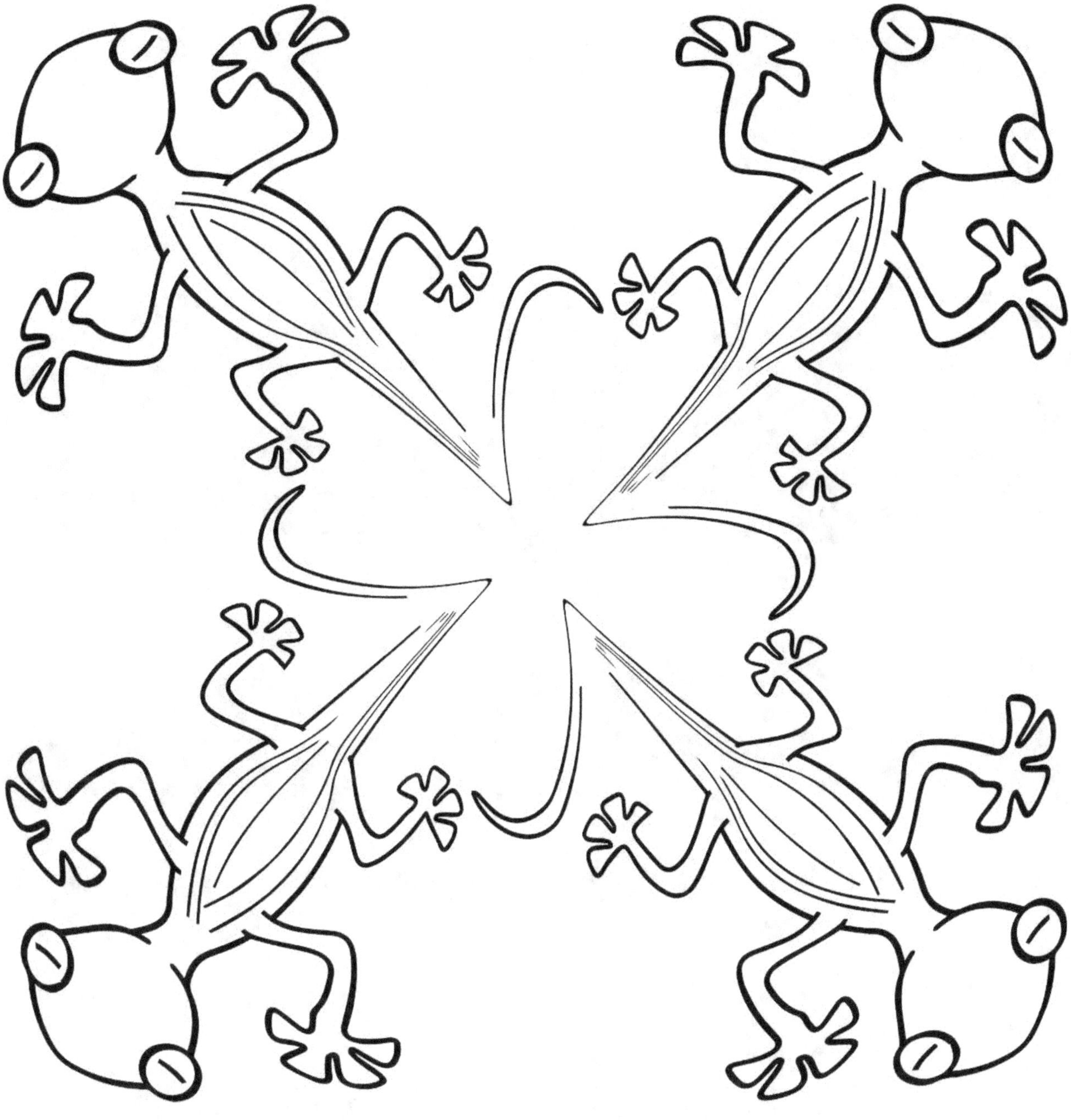

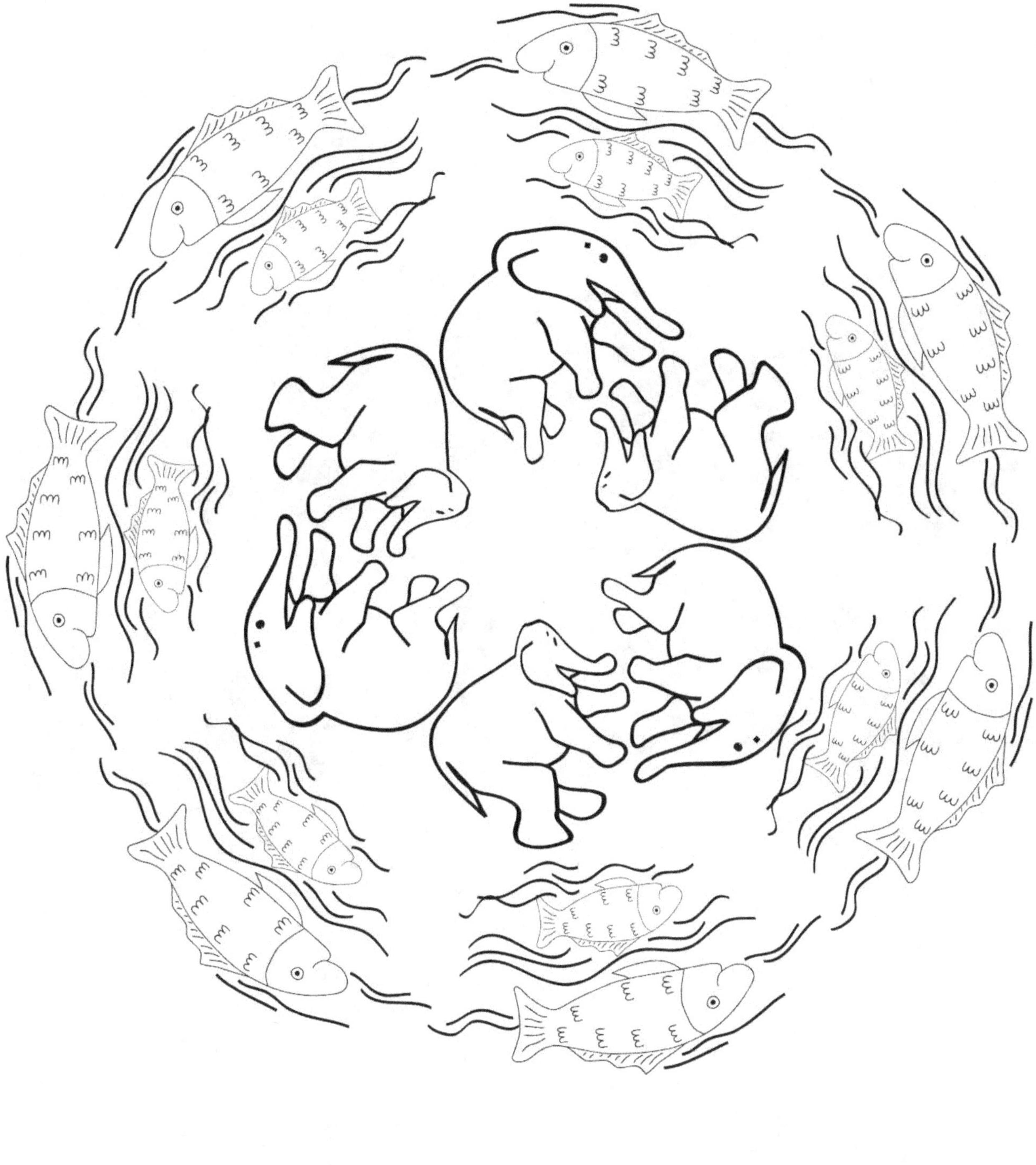

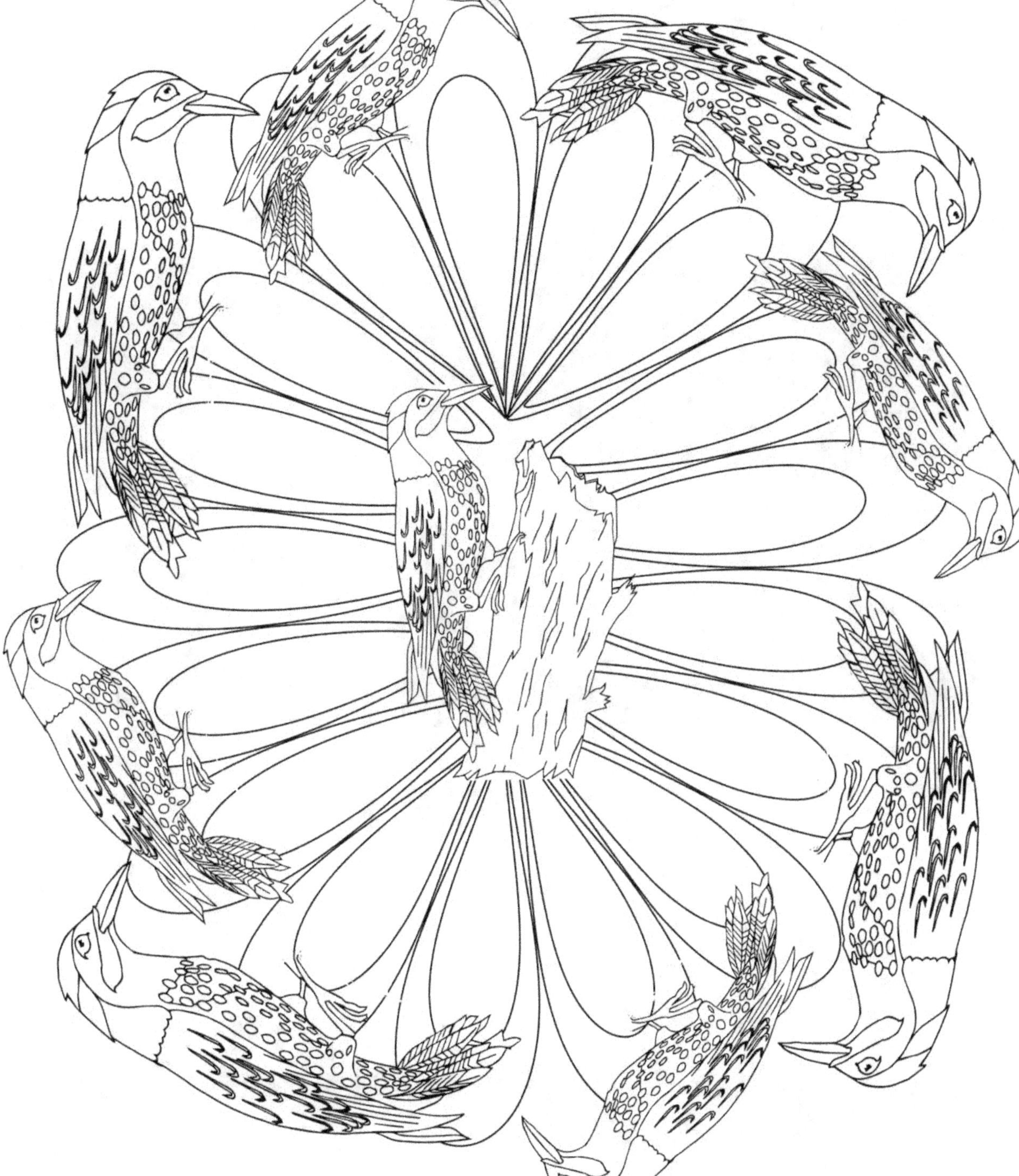

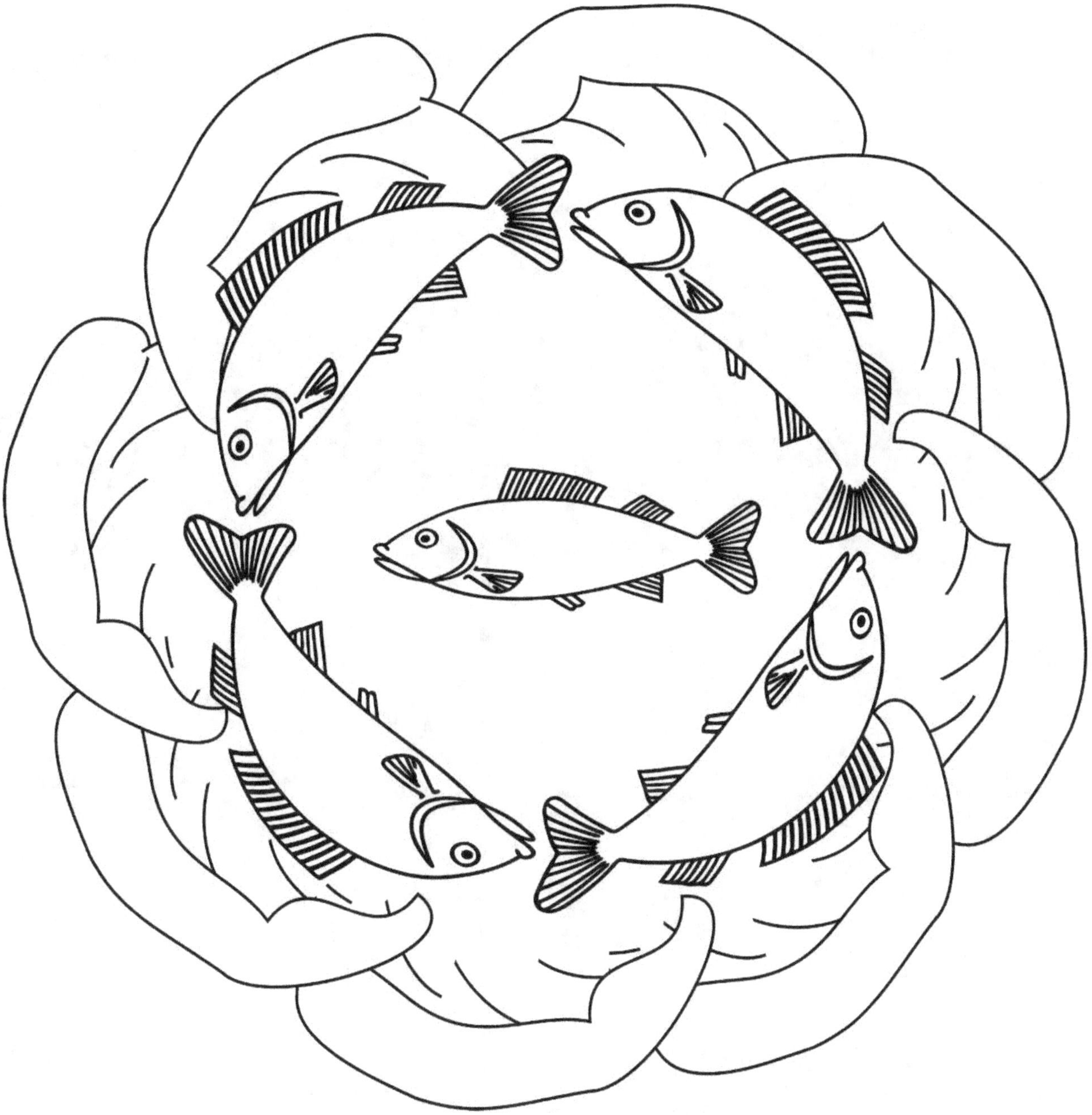

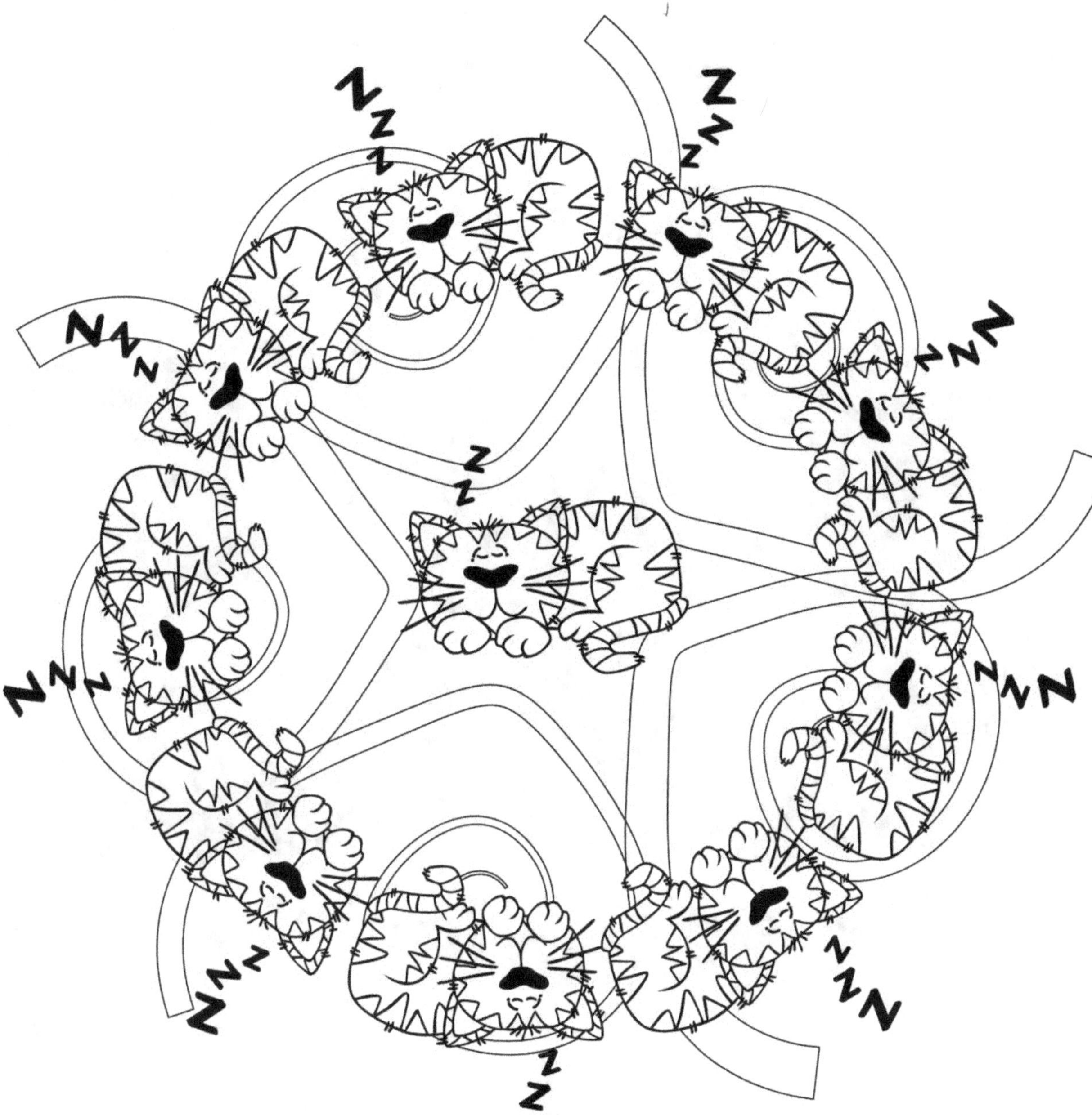
ZZZ
ZZZ
ZZZ
ZZZ
ZZZ
ZZZ
ZZZ
ZZZ
ZZZ
ZZZ
ZZZ

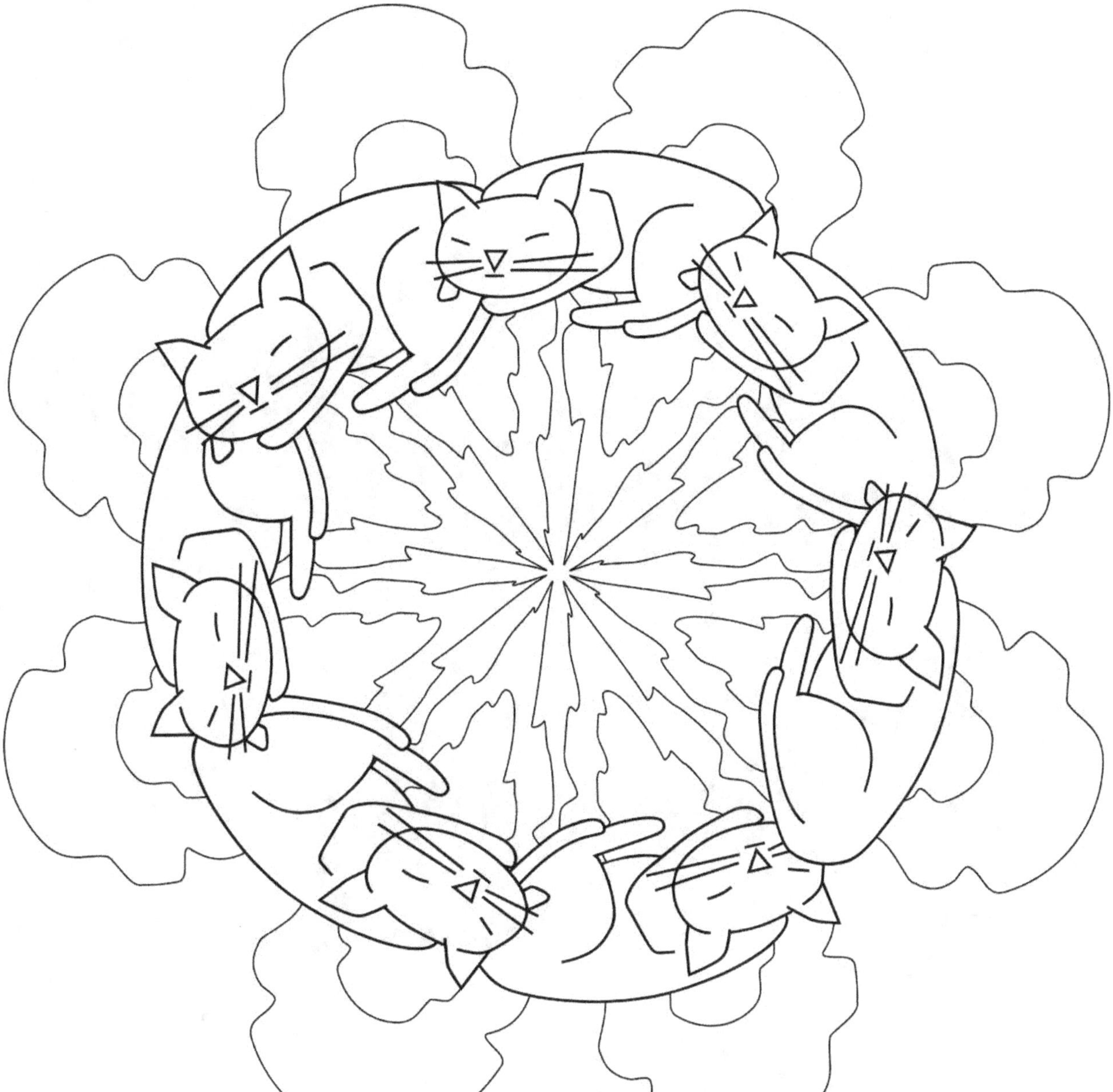

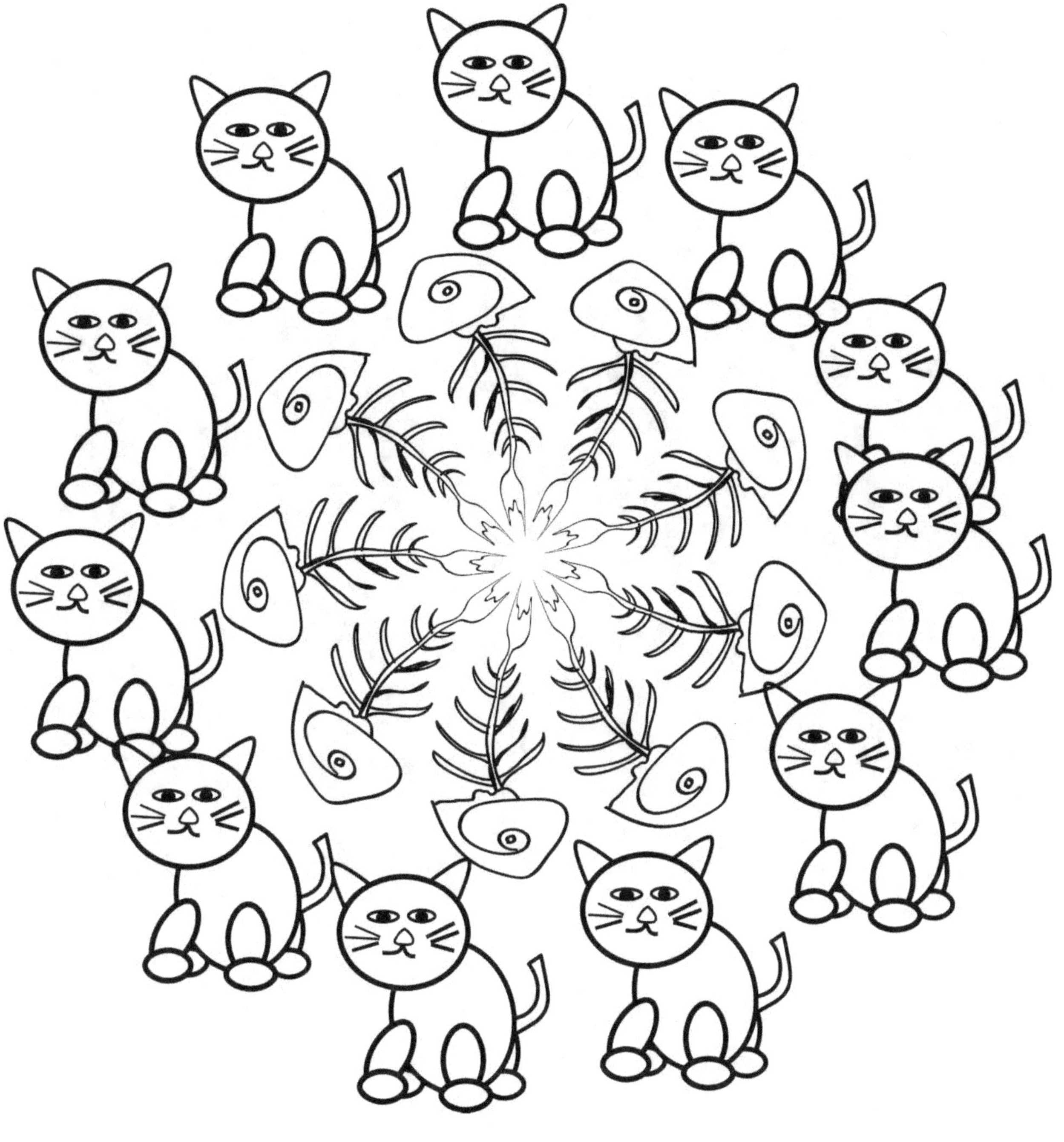

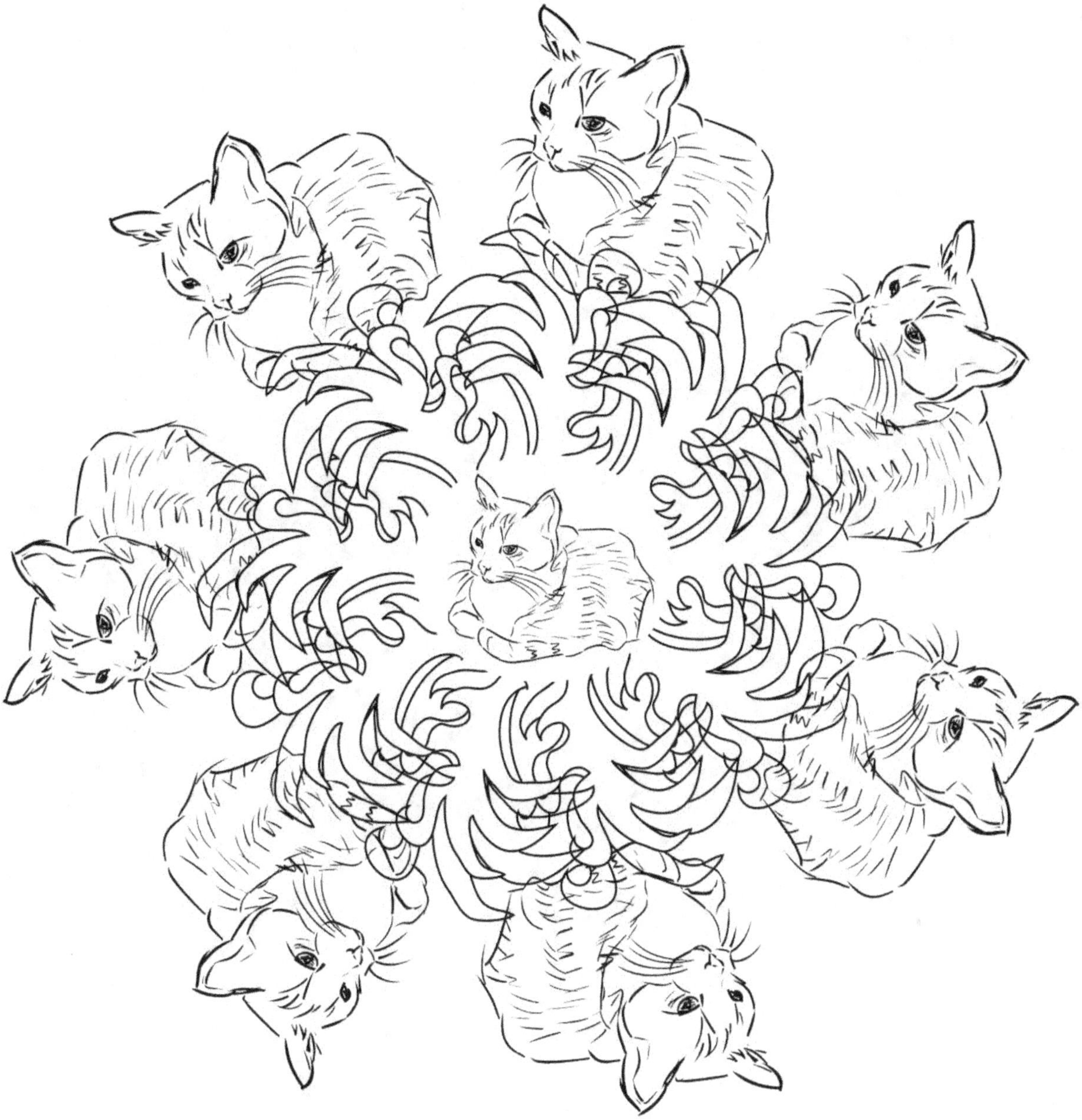

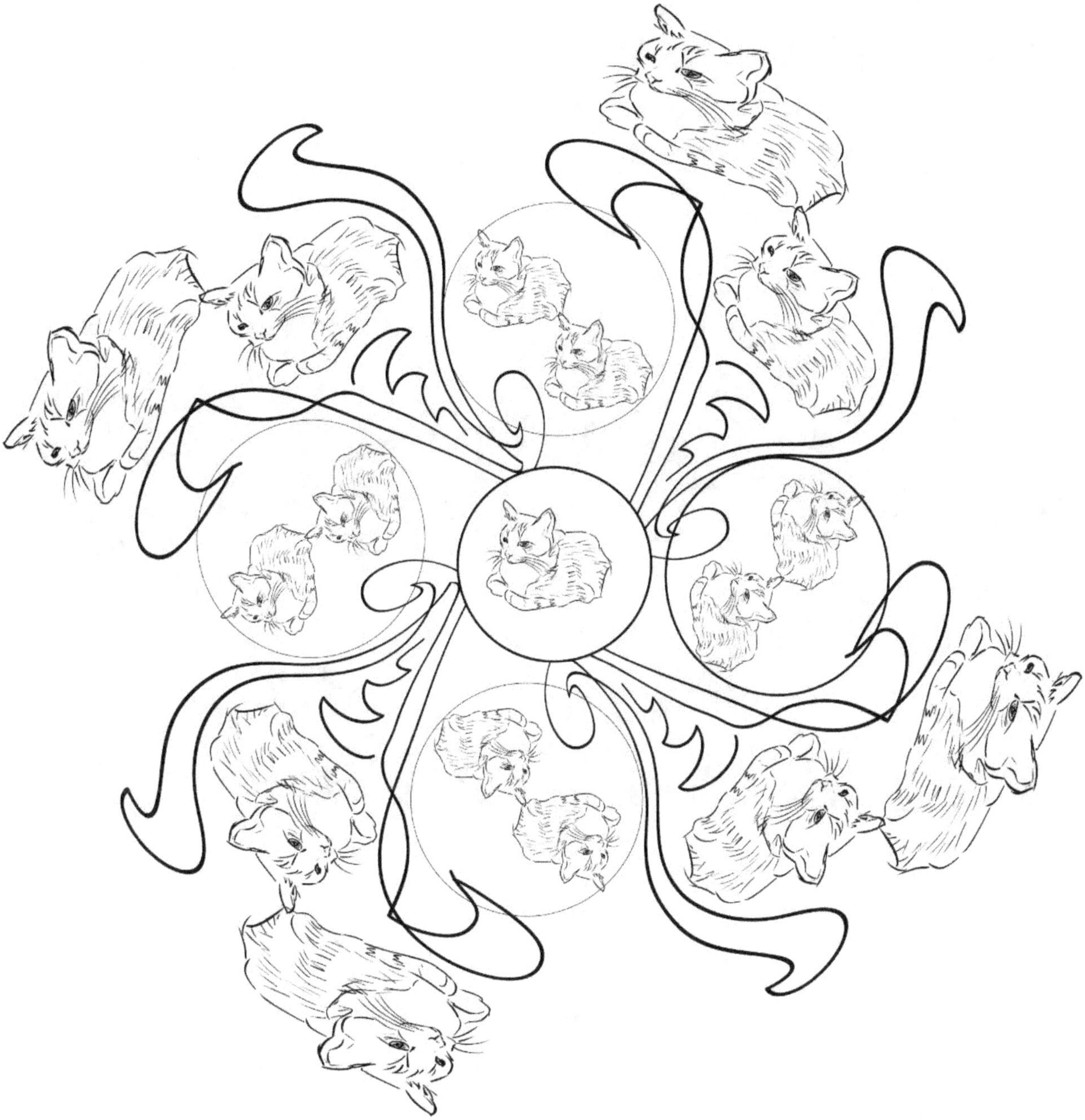

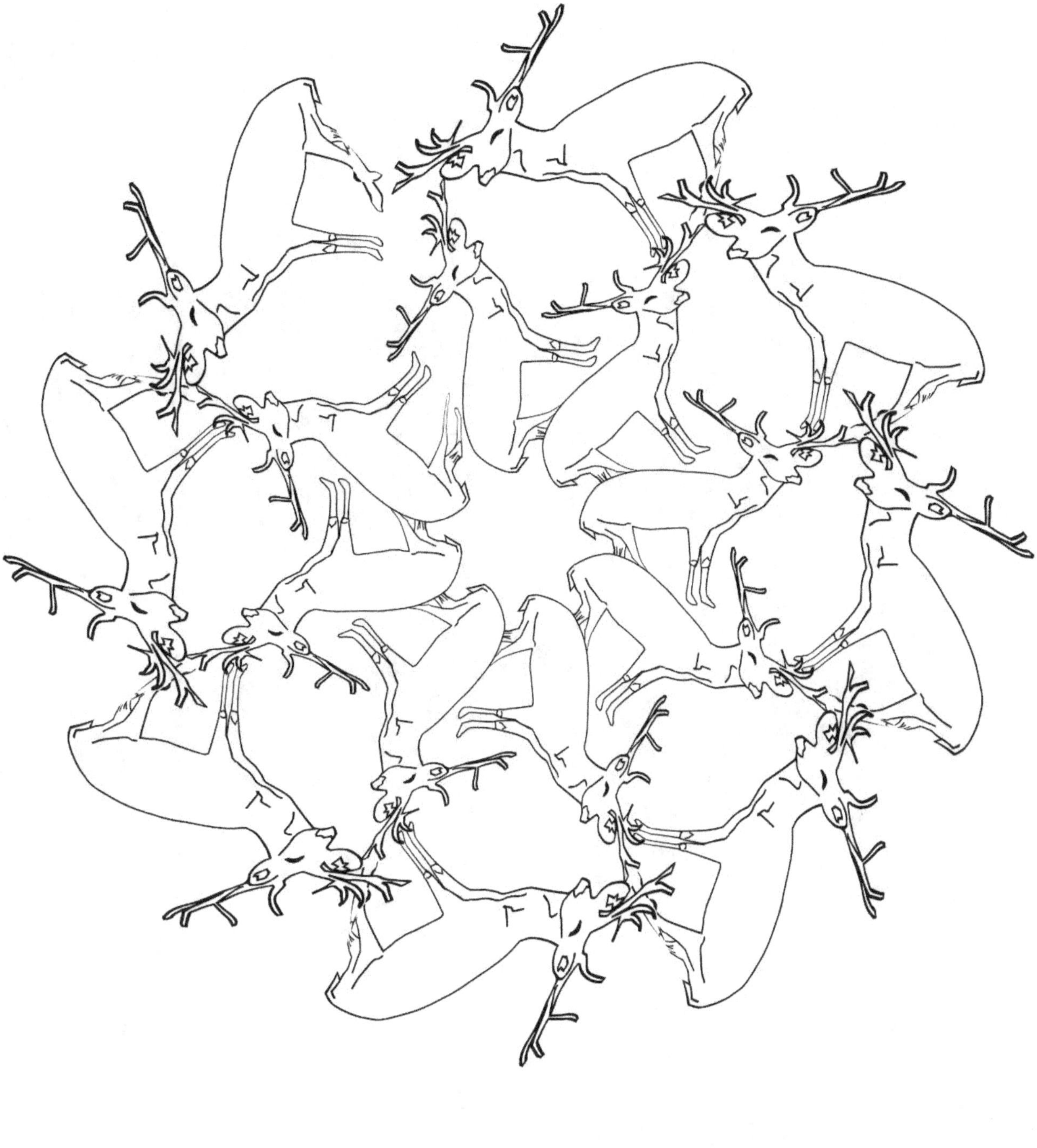

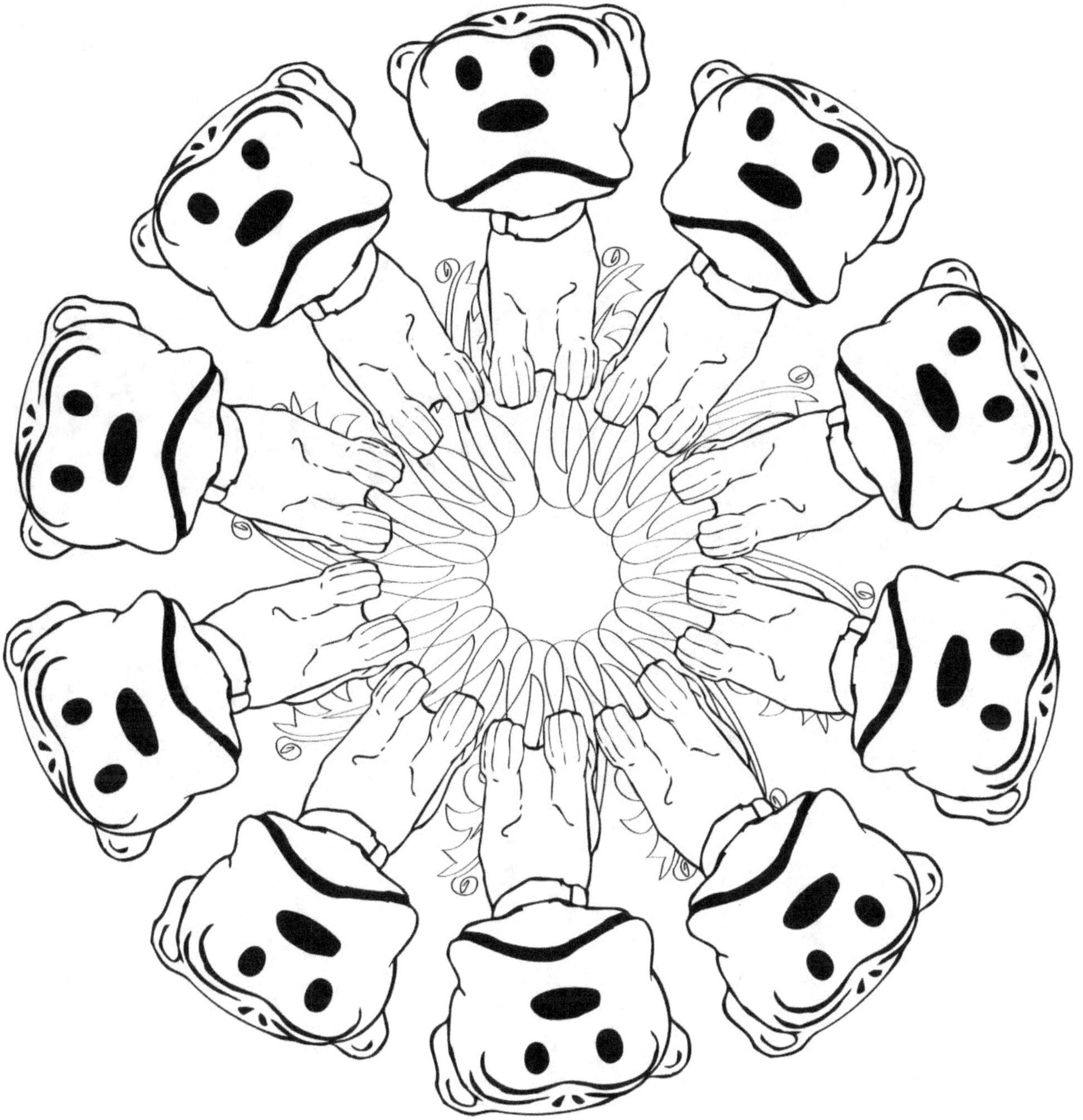

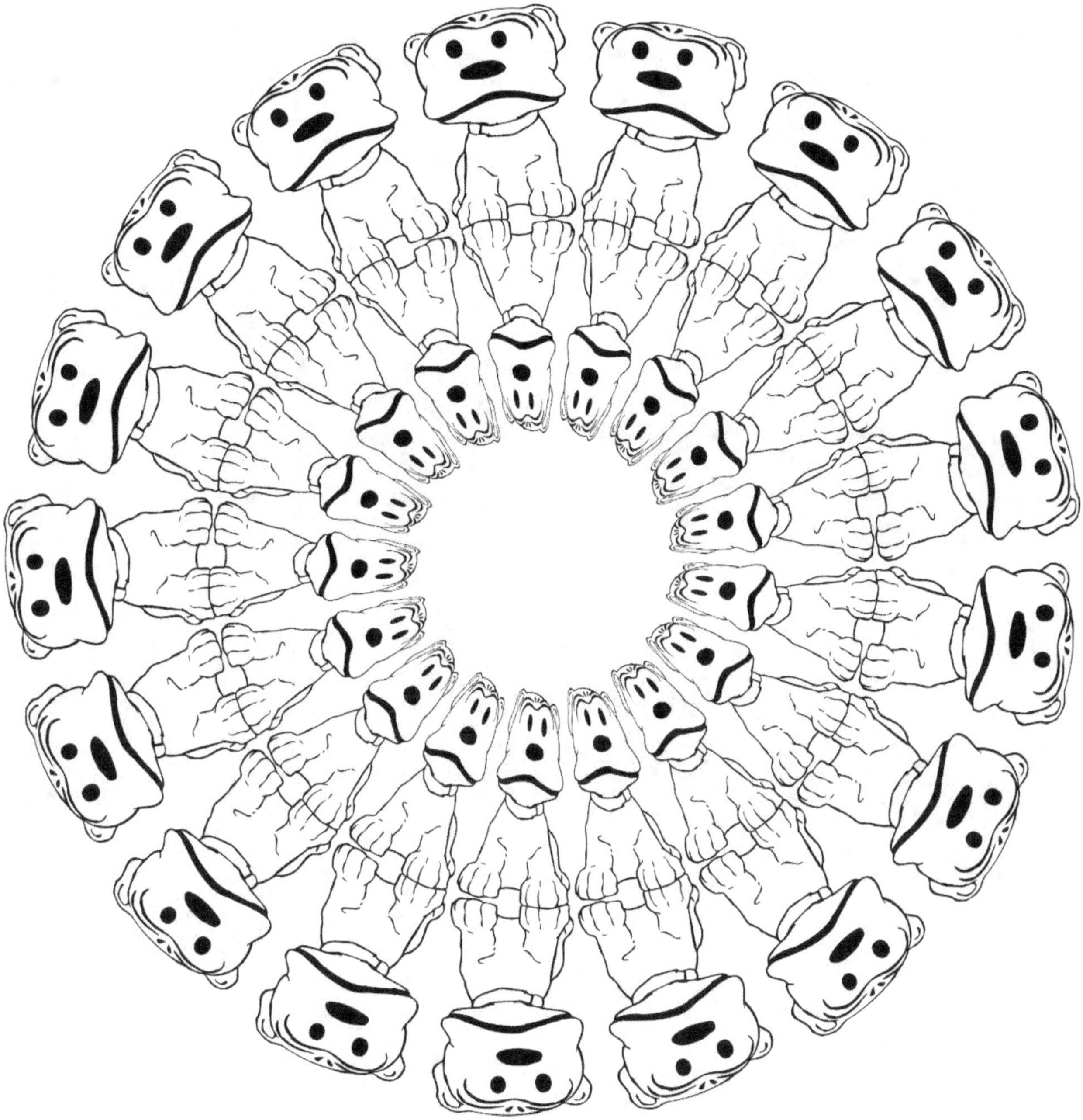

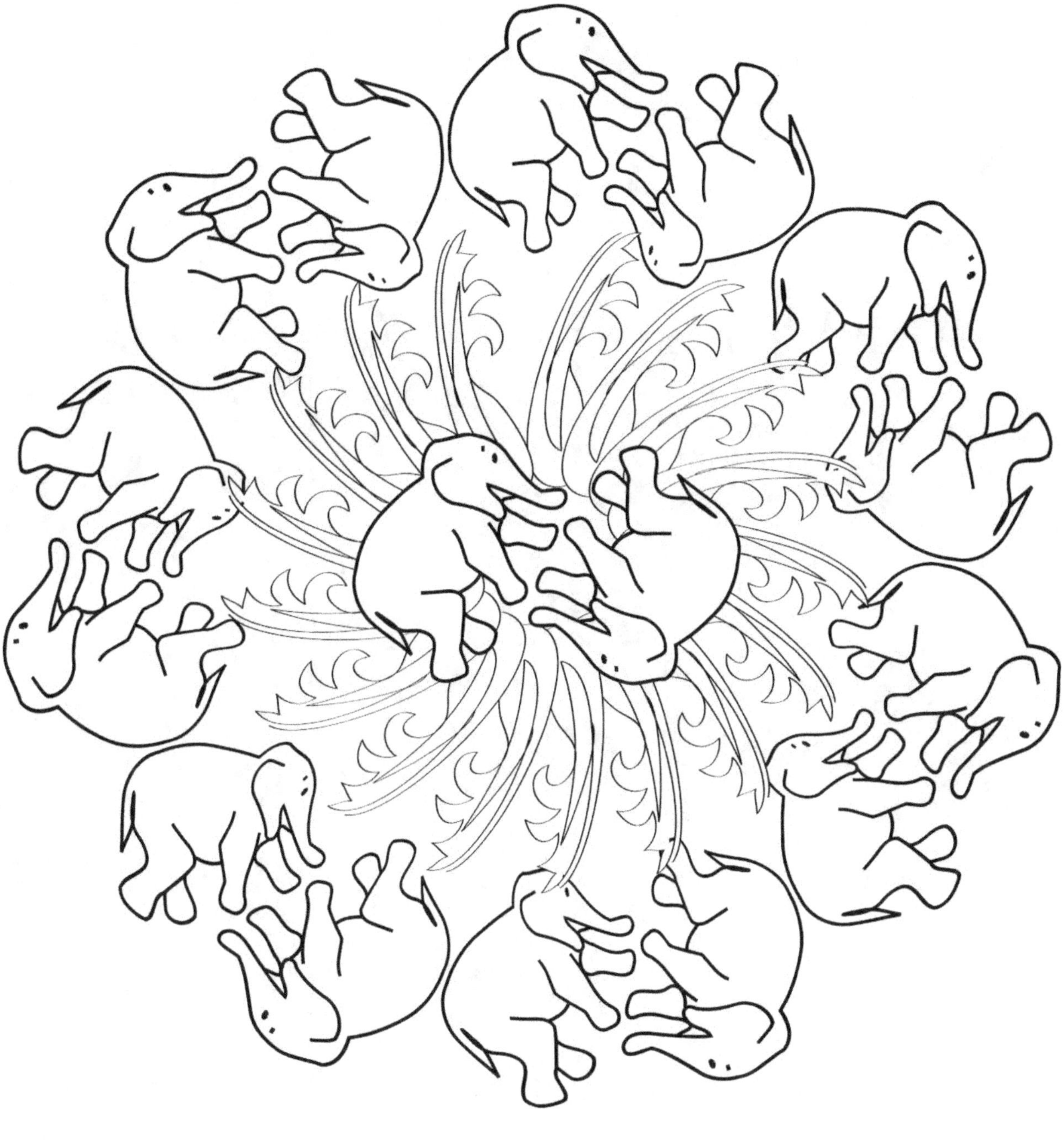

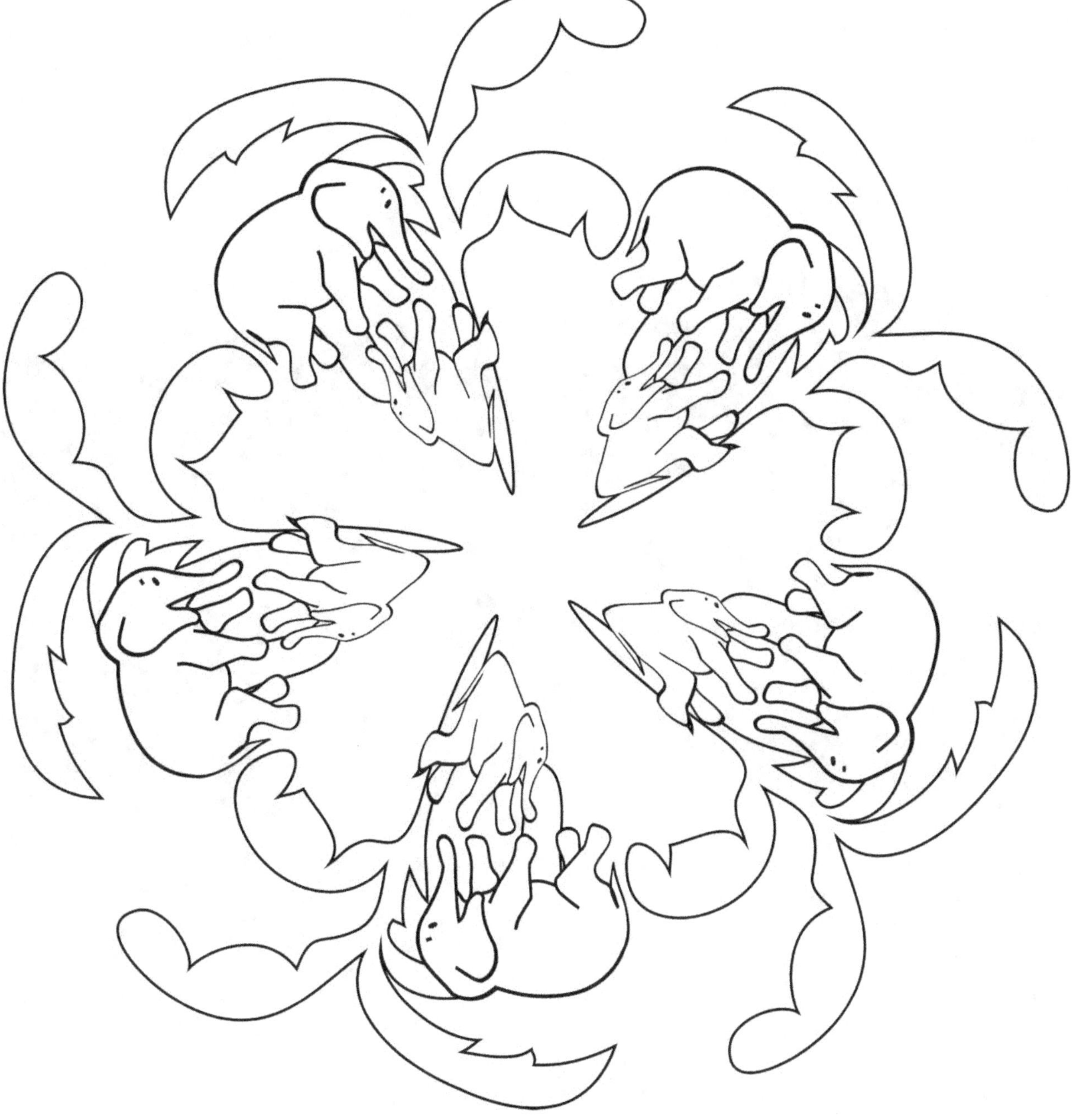

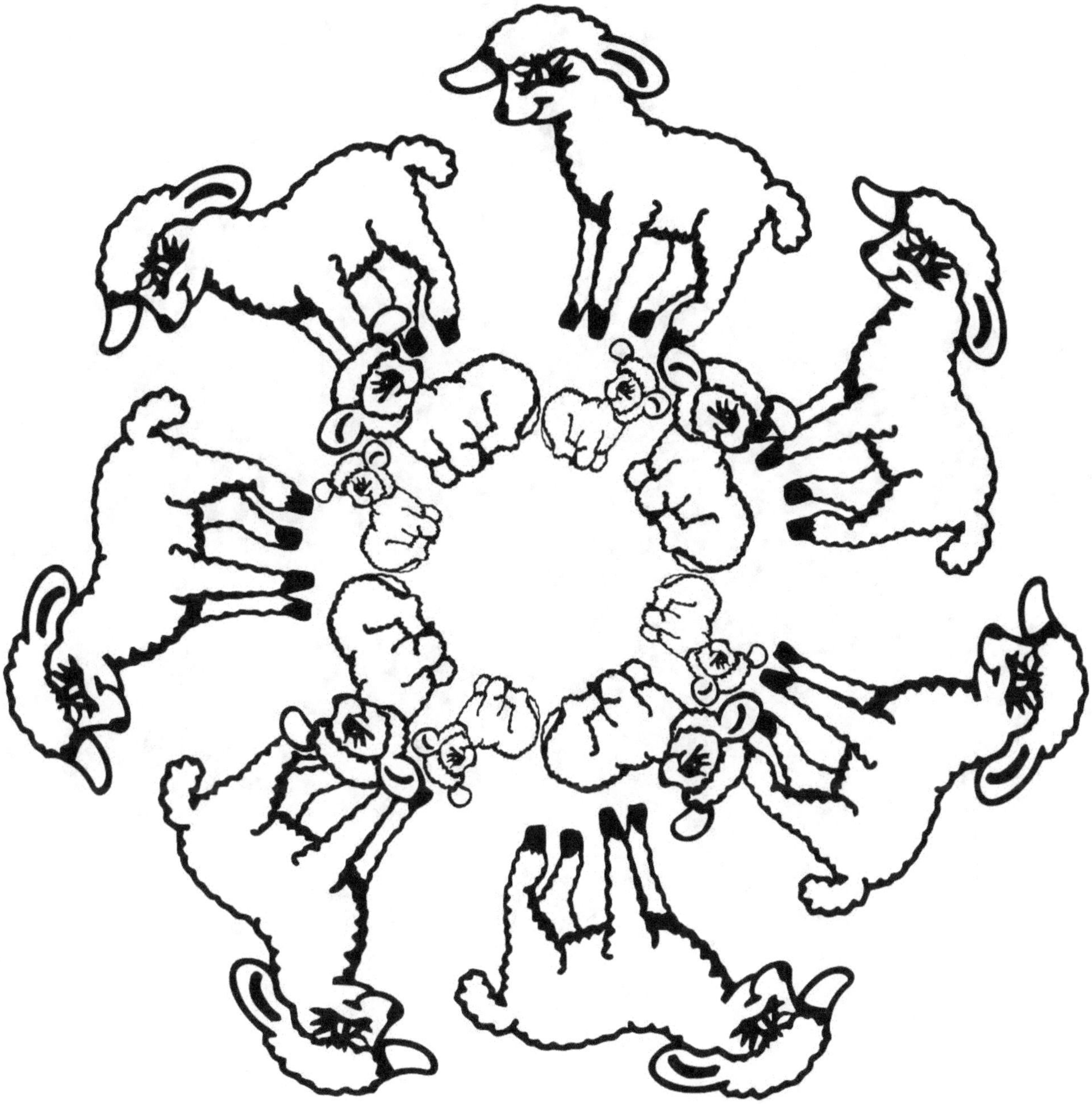

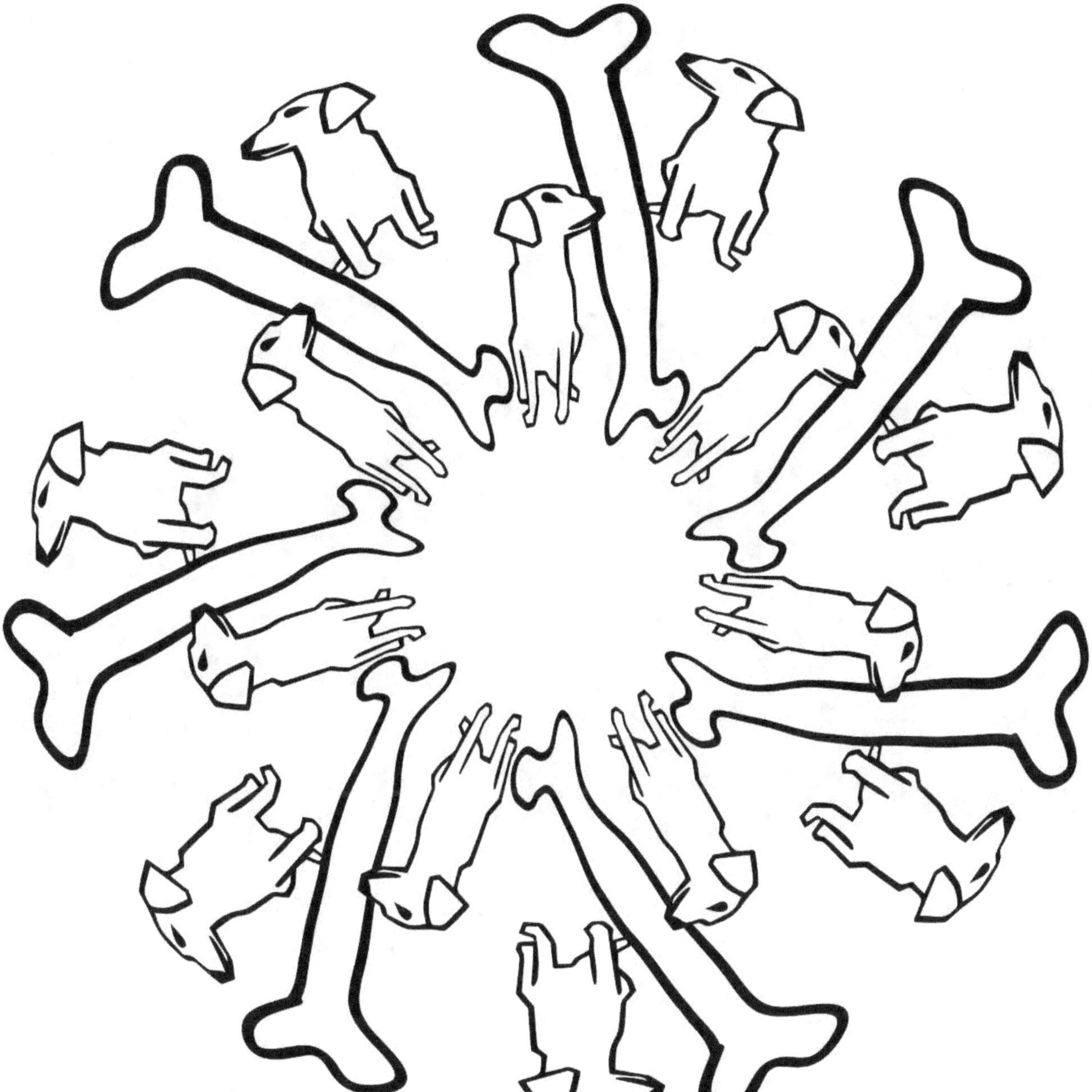

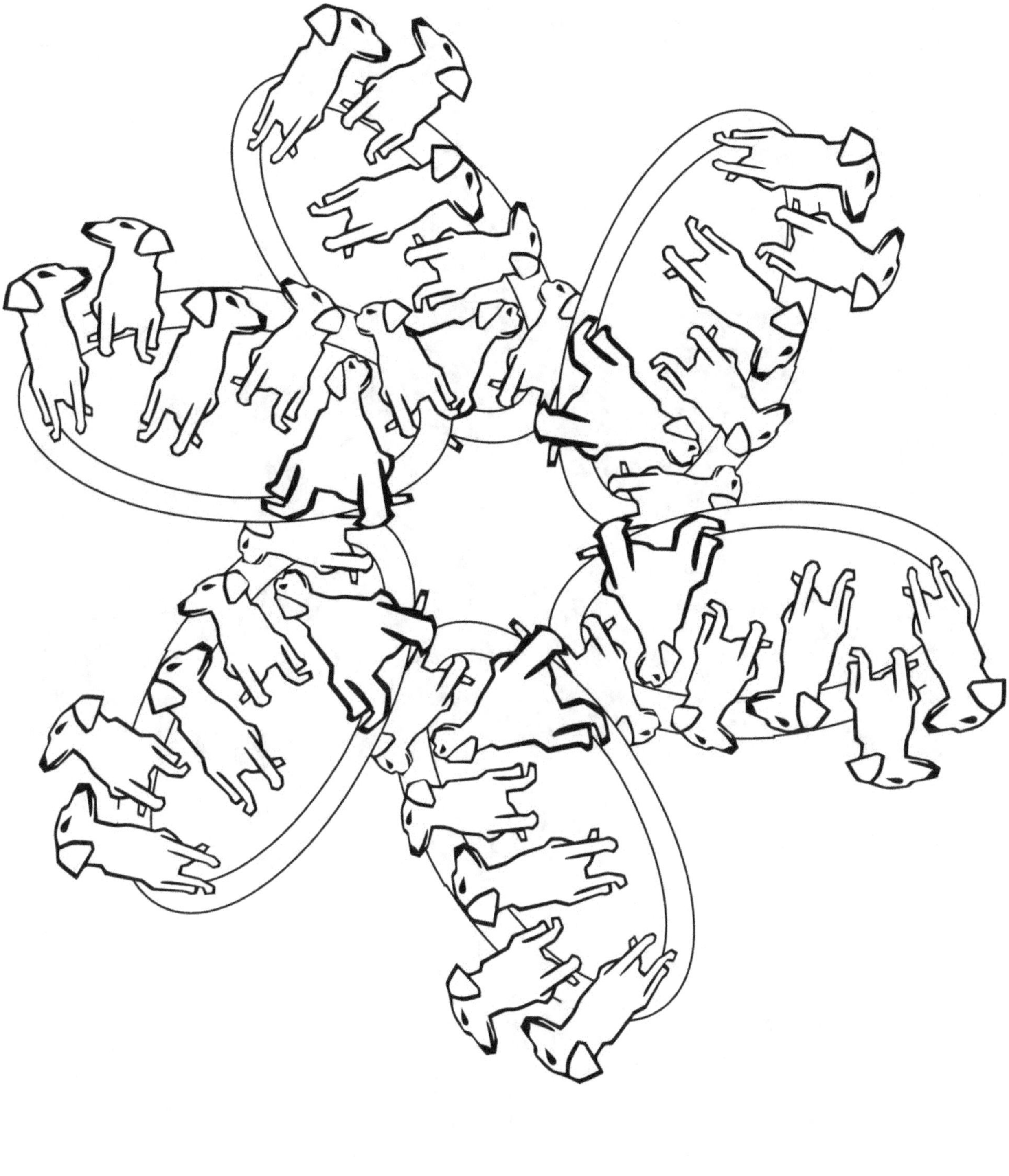

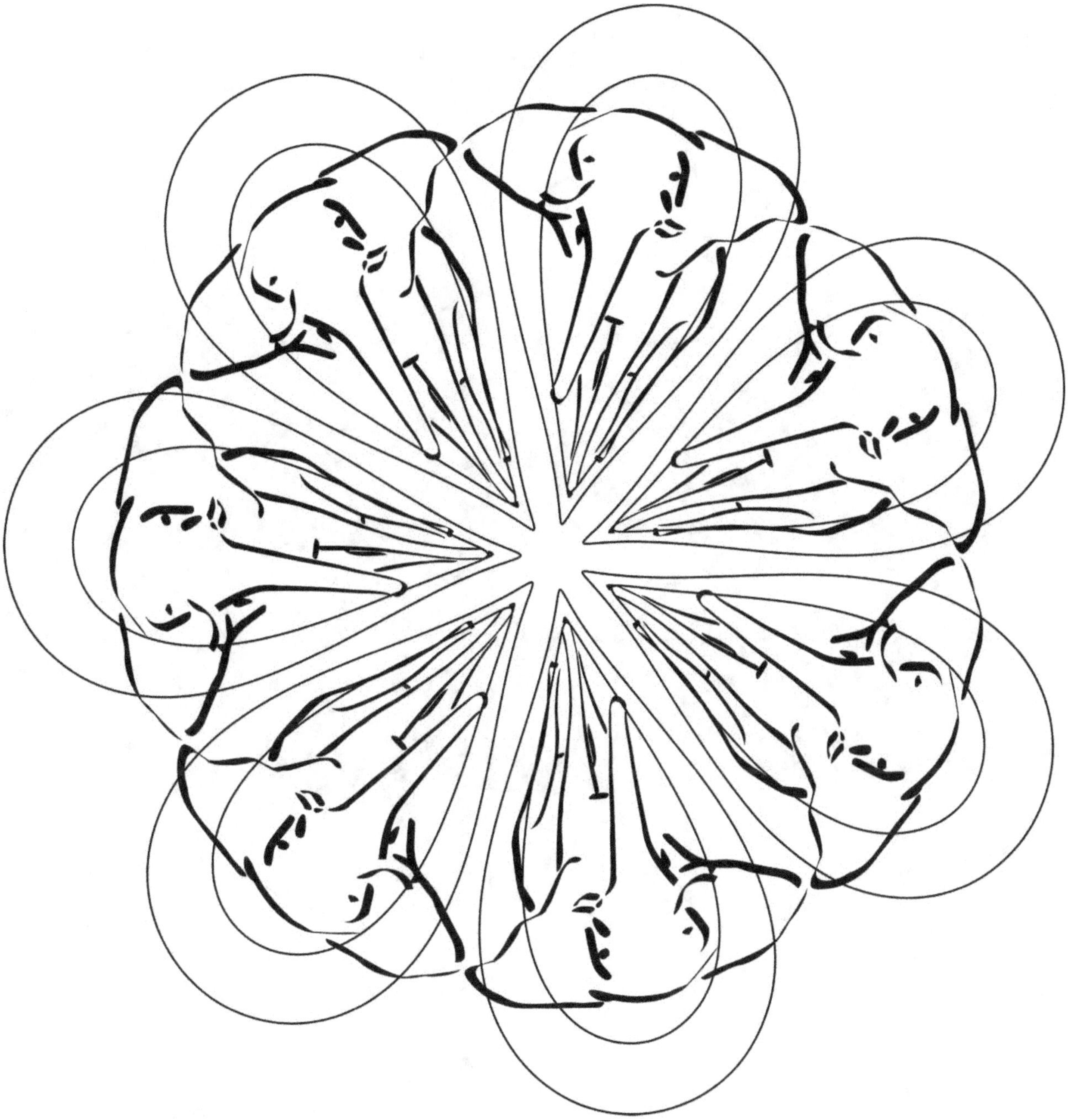

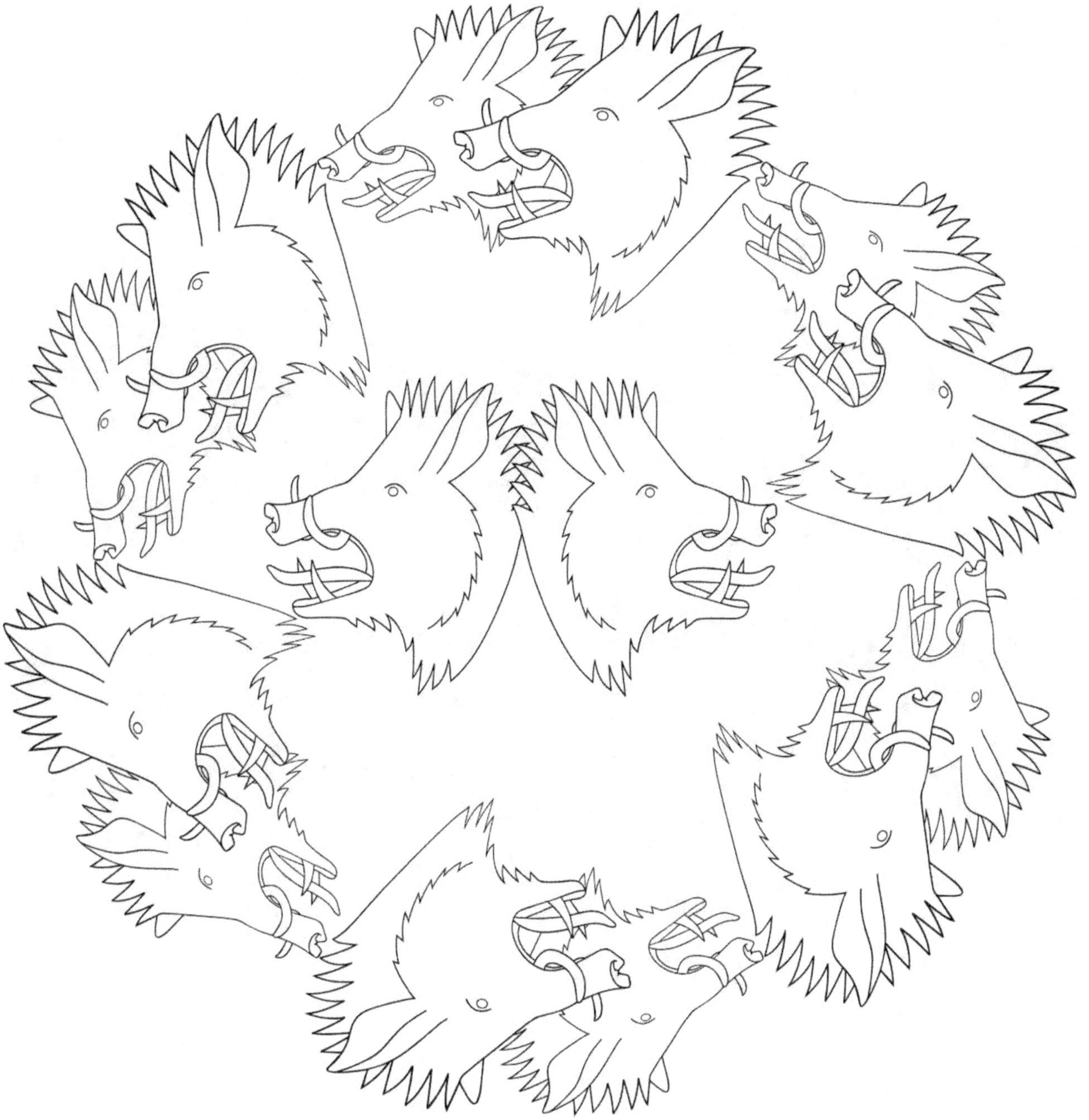

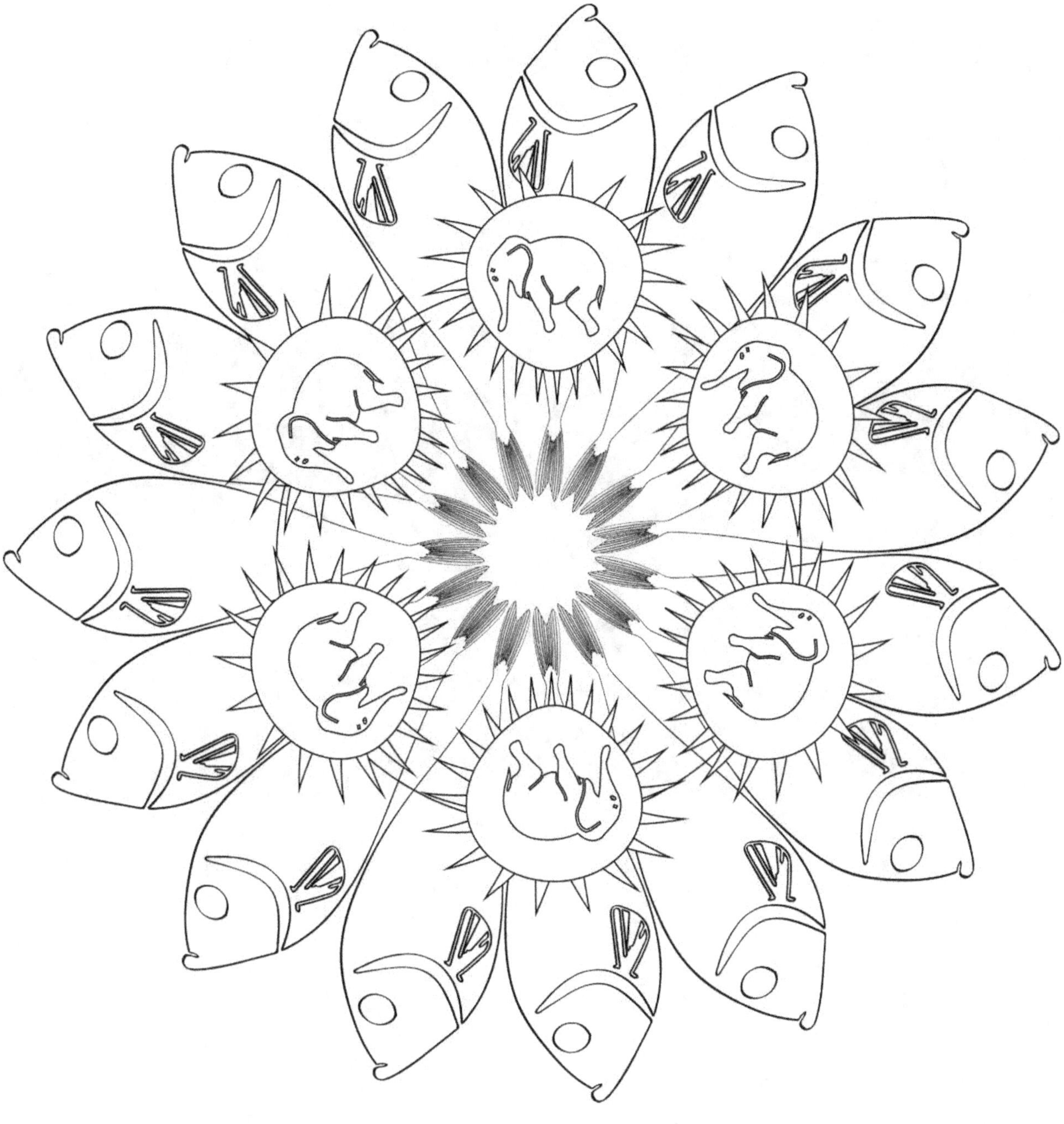

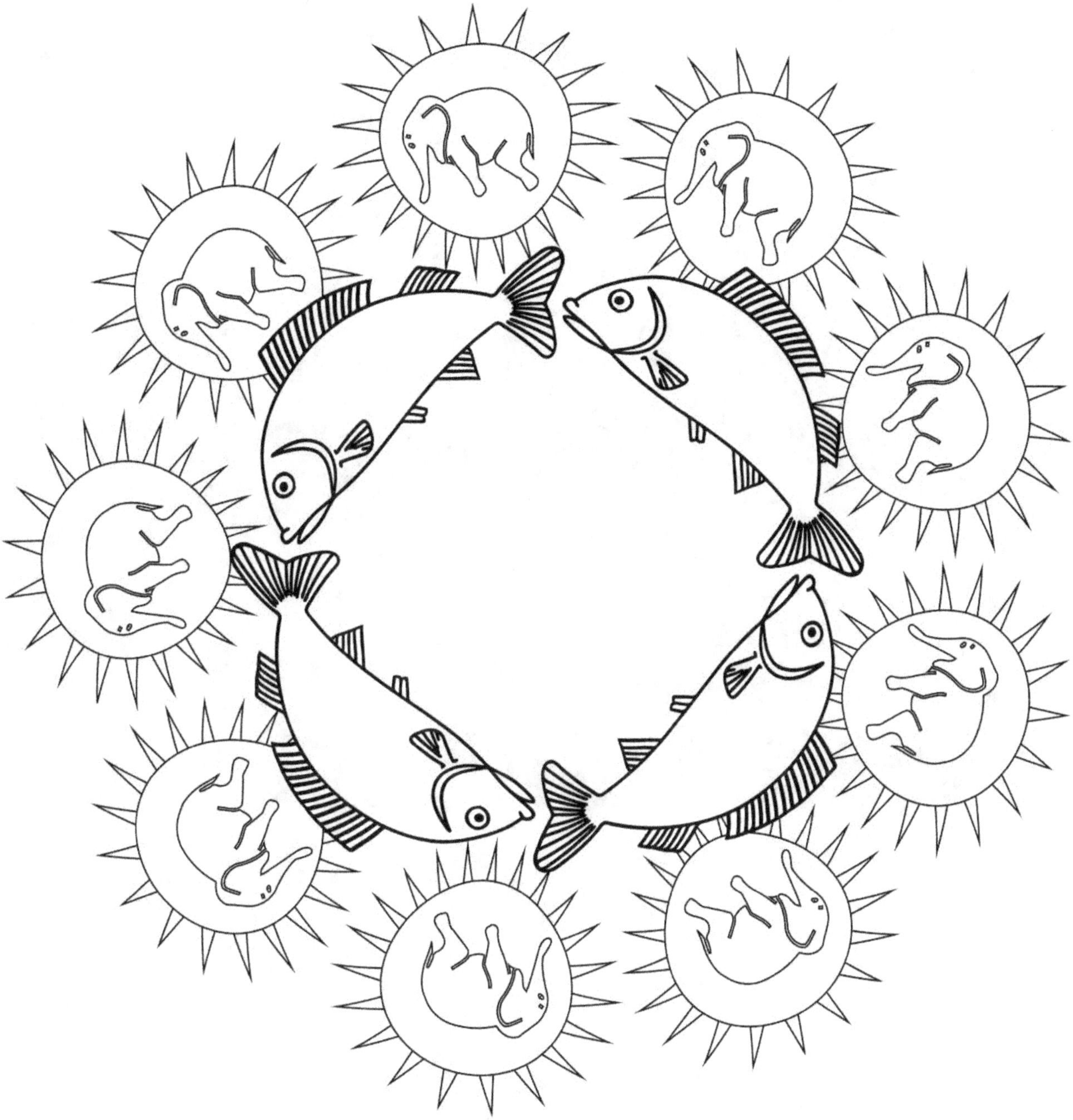

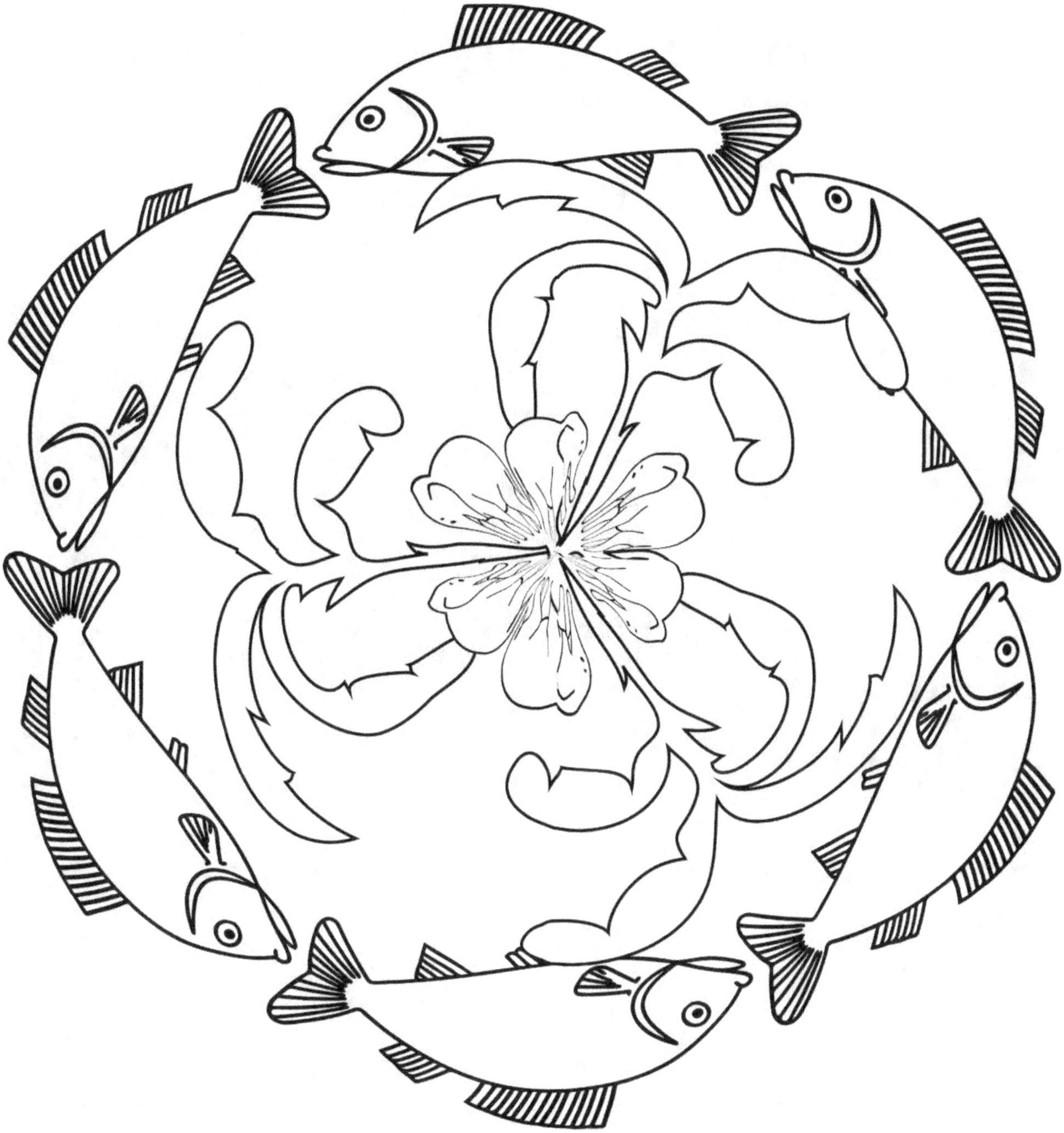

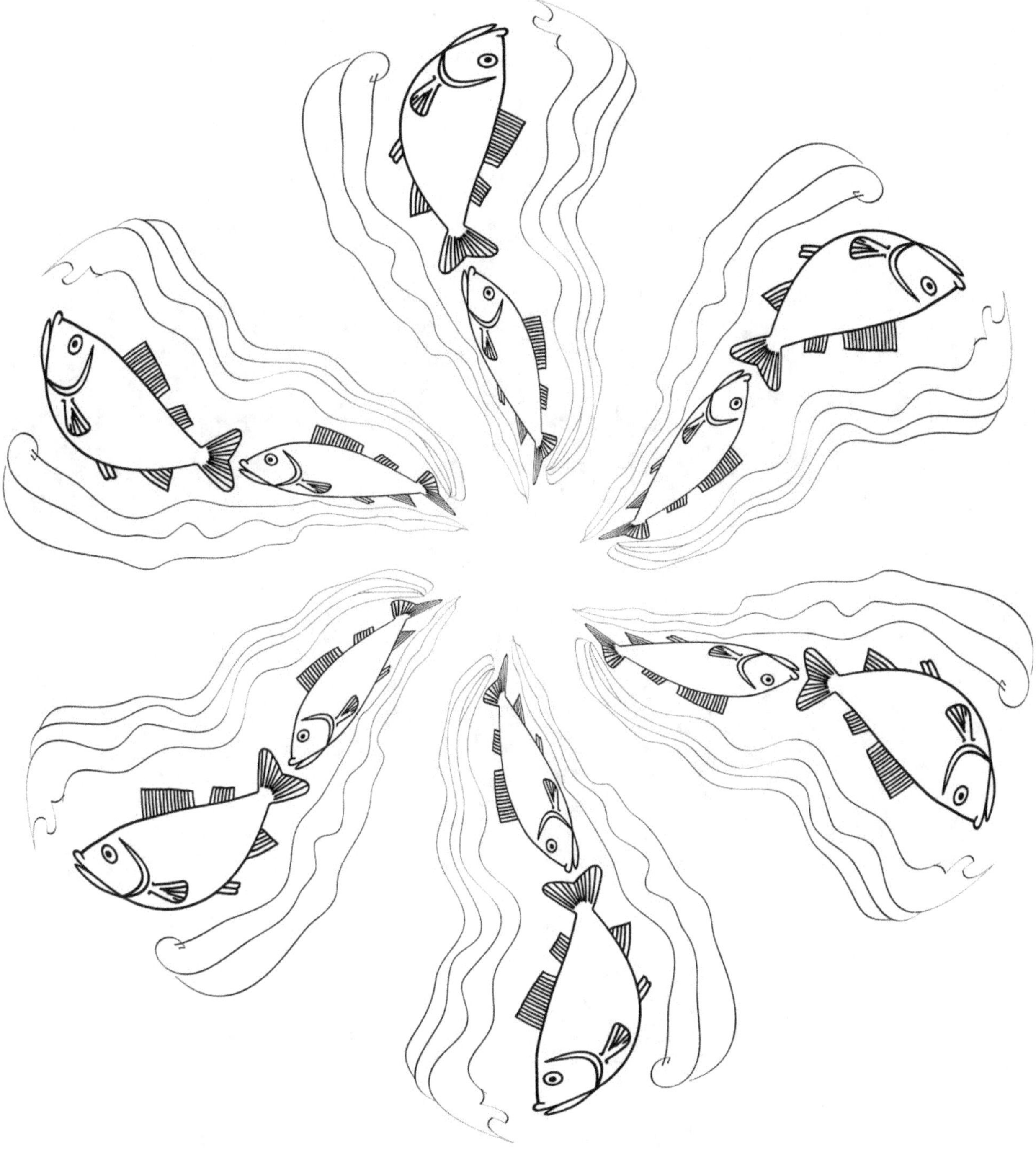

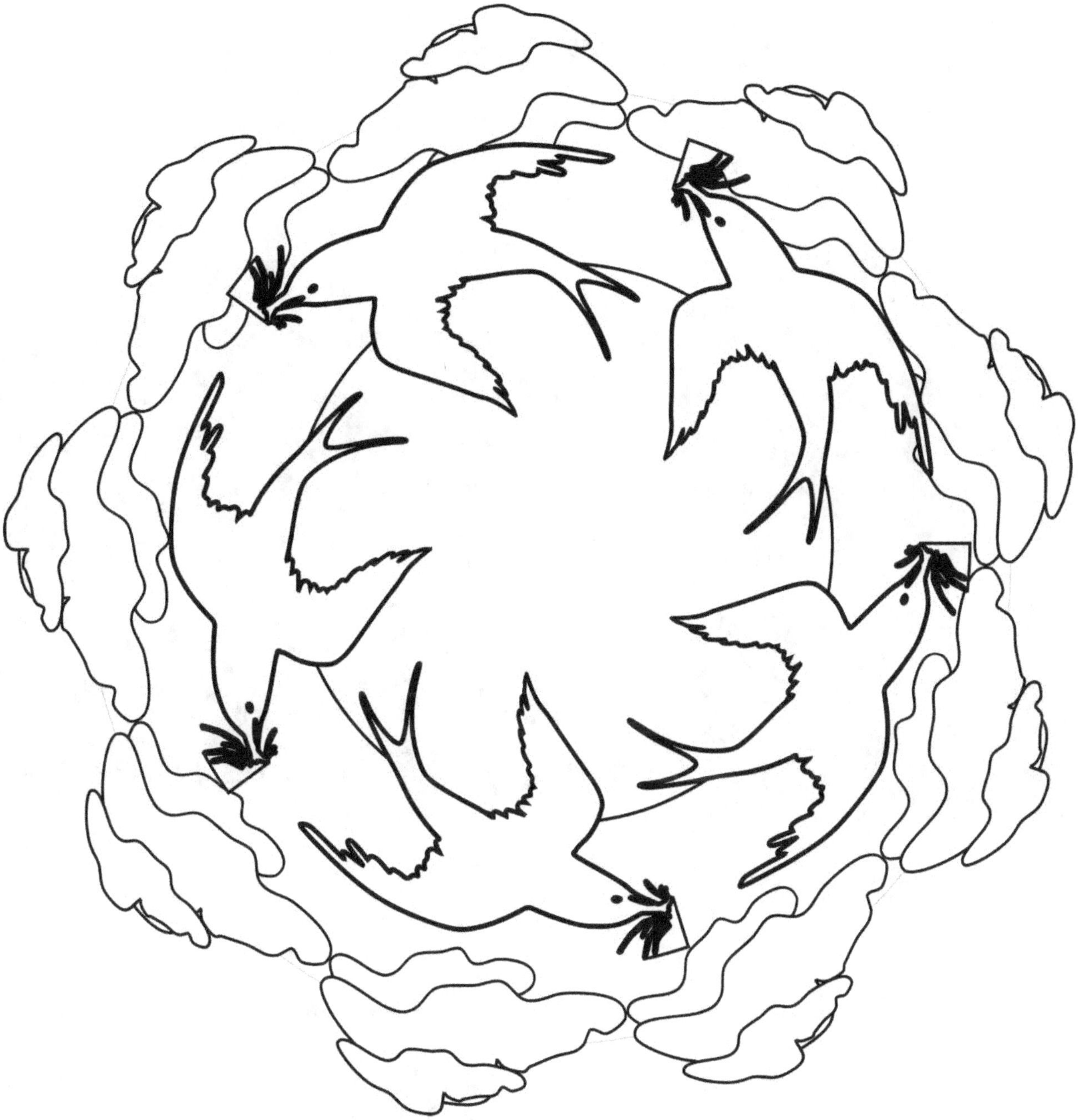

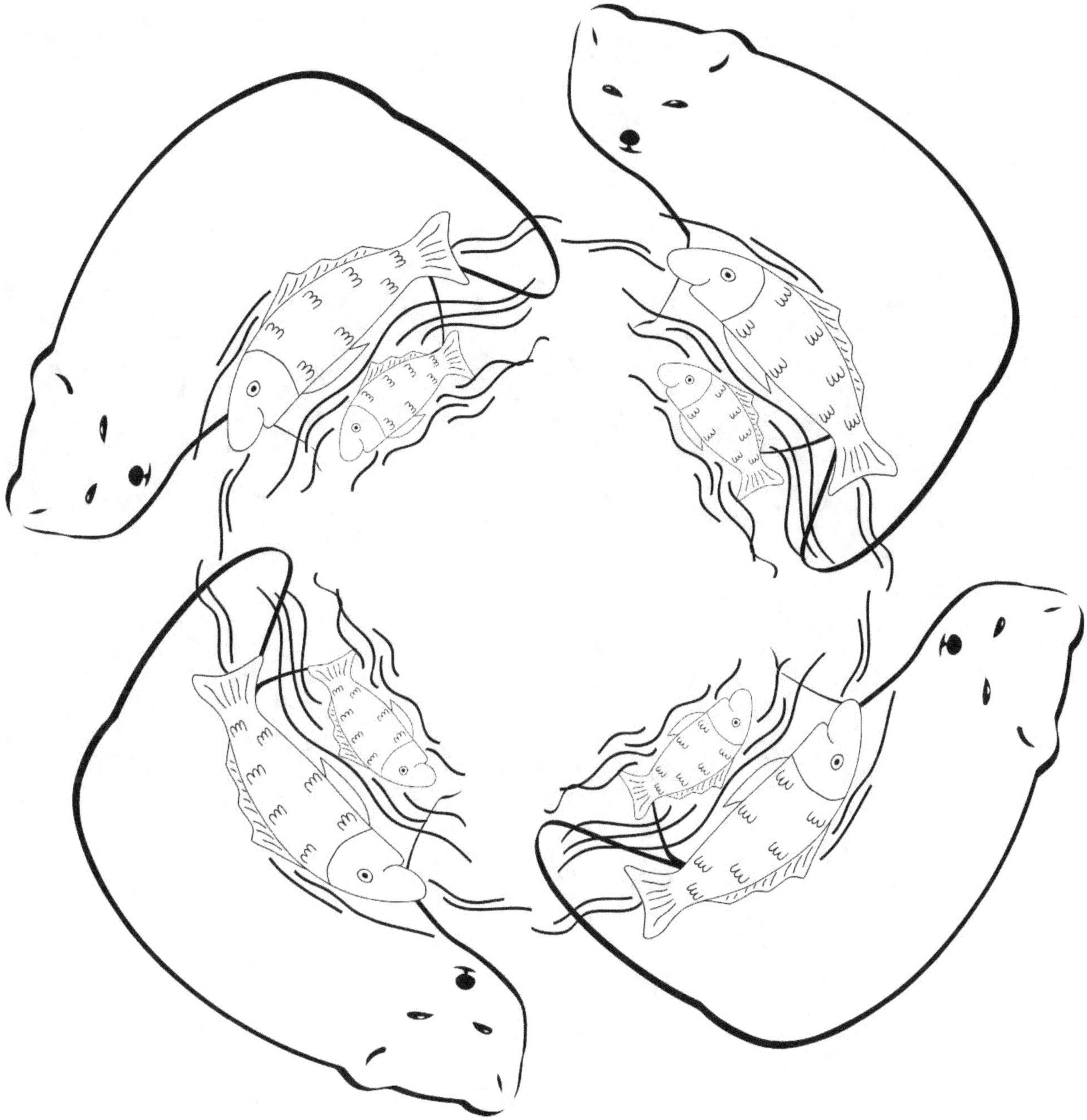

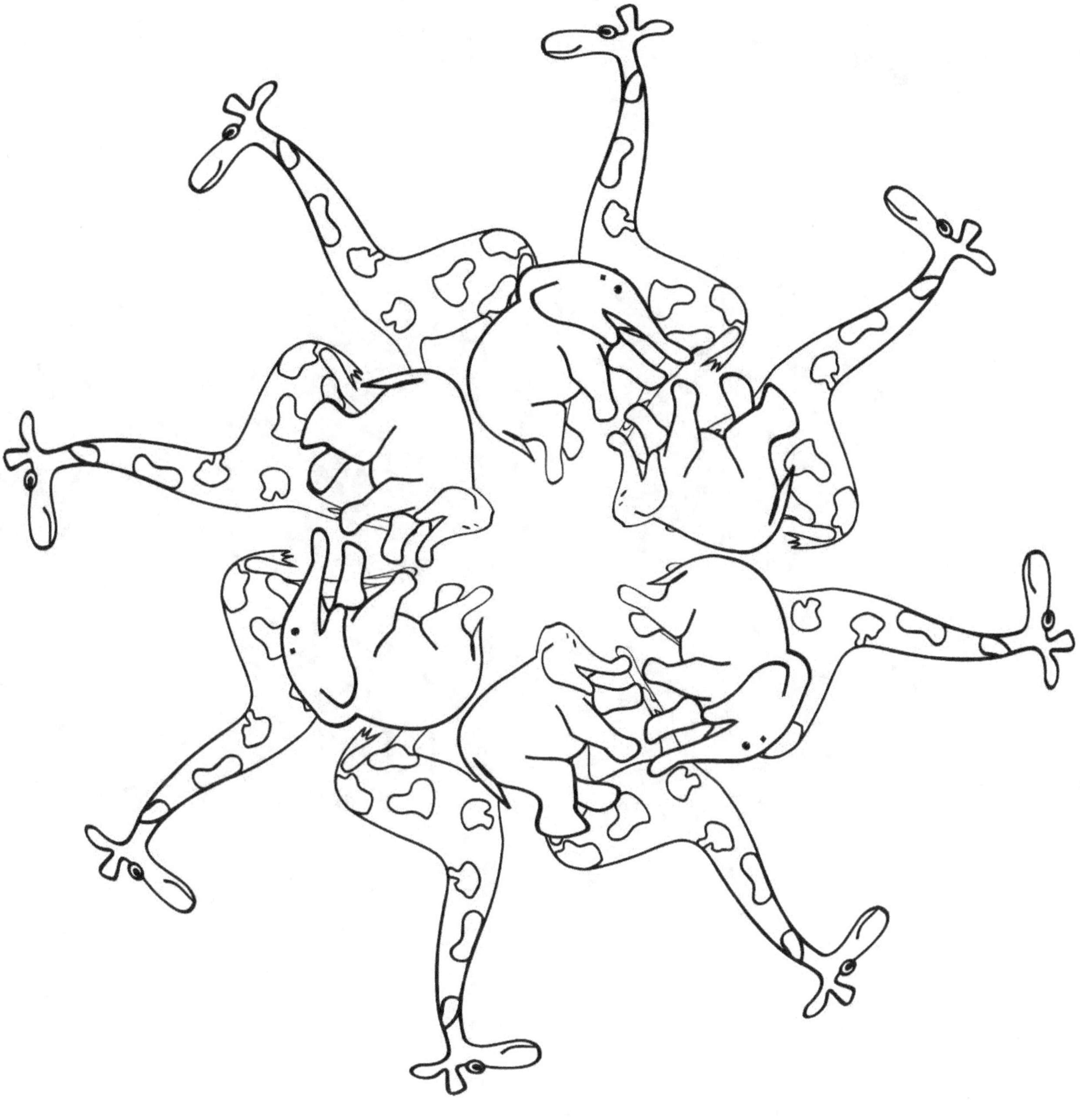

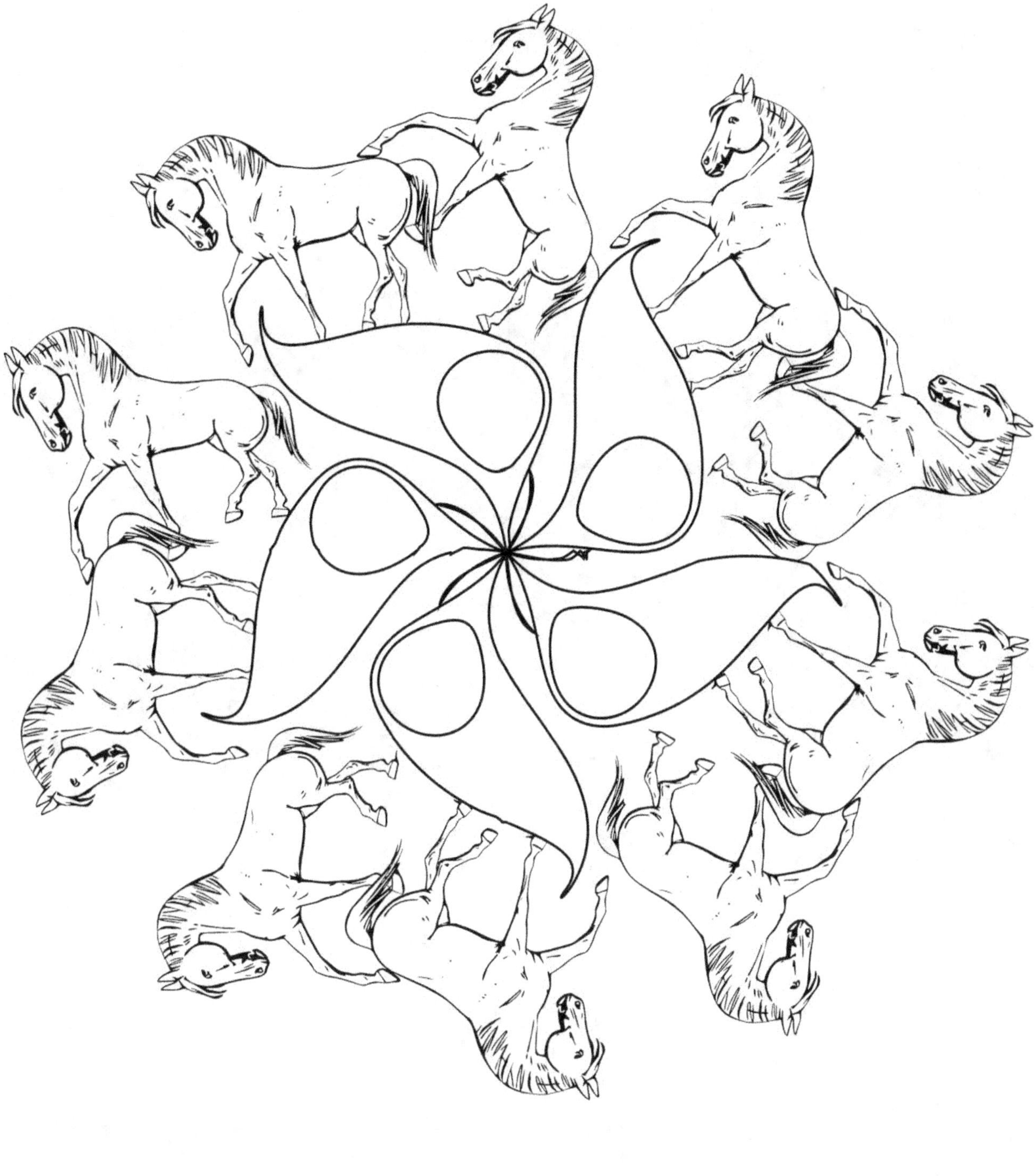

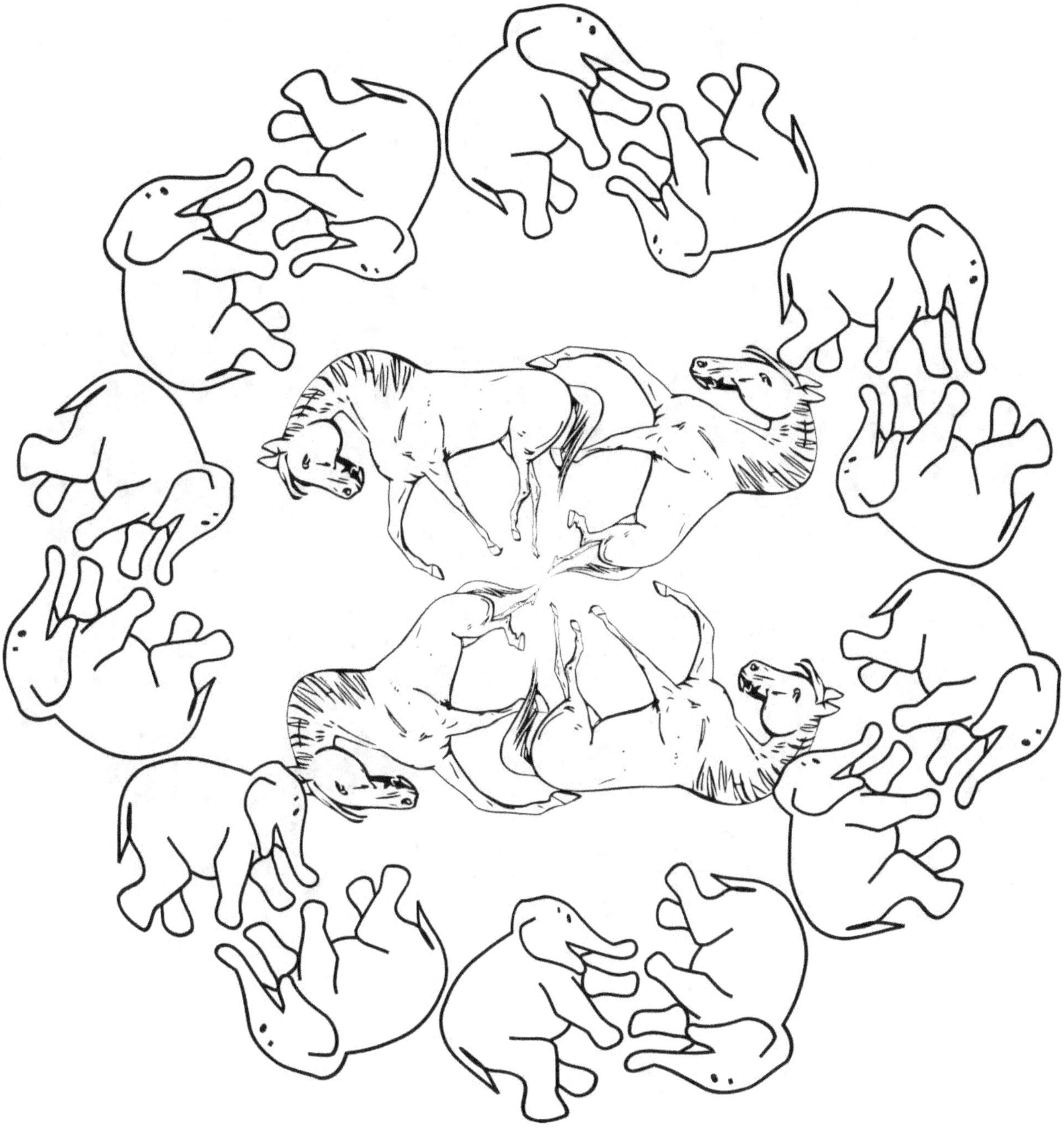

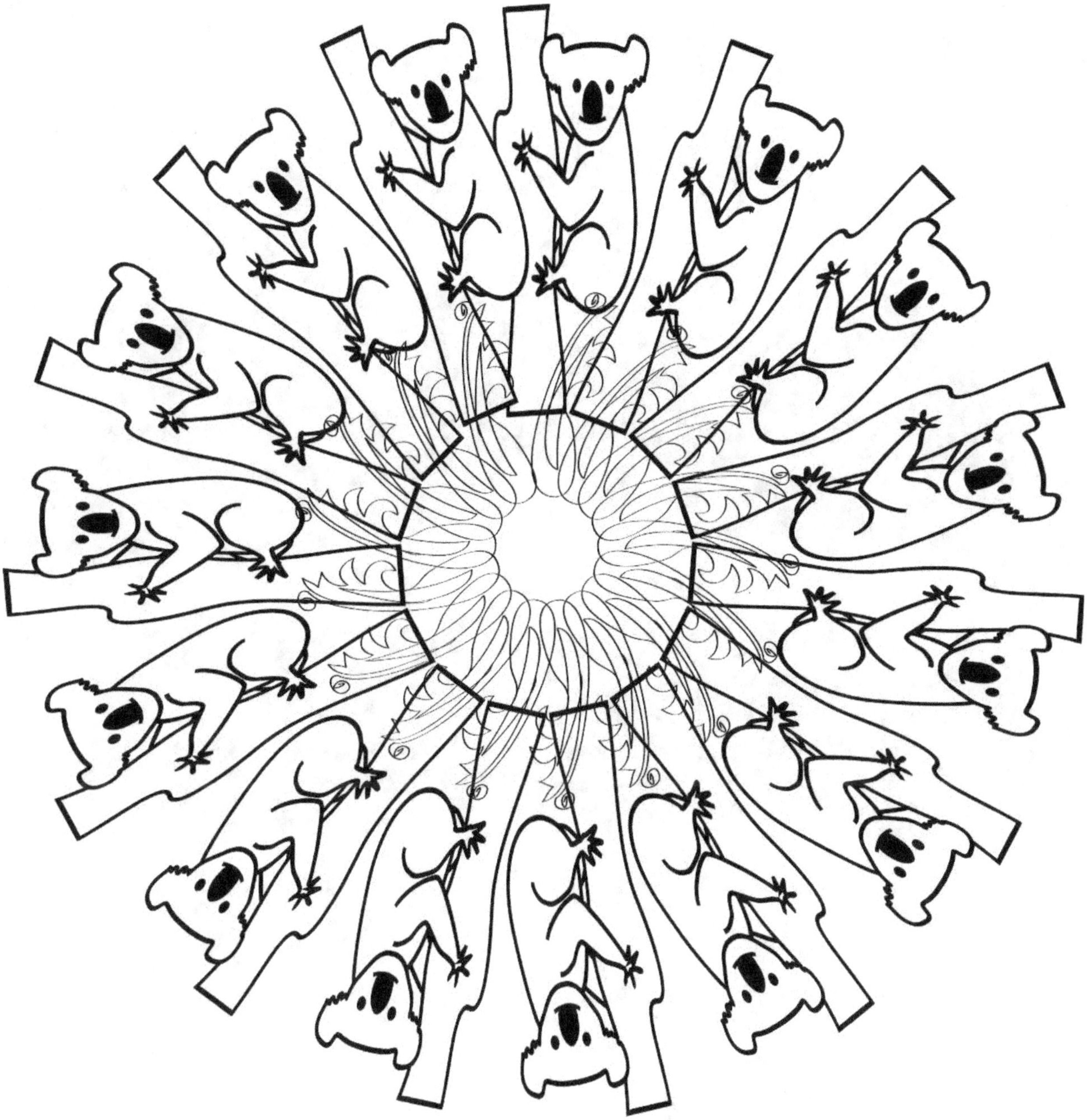

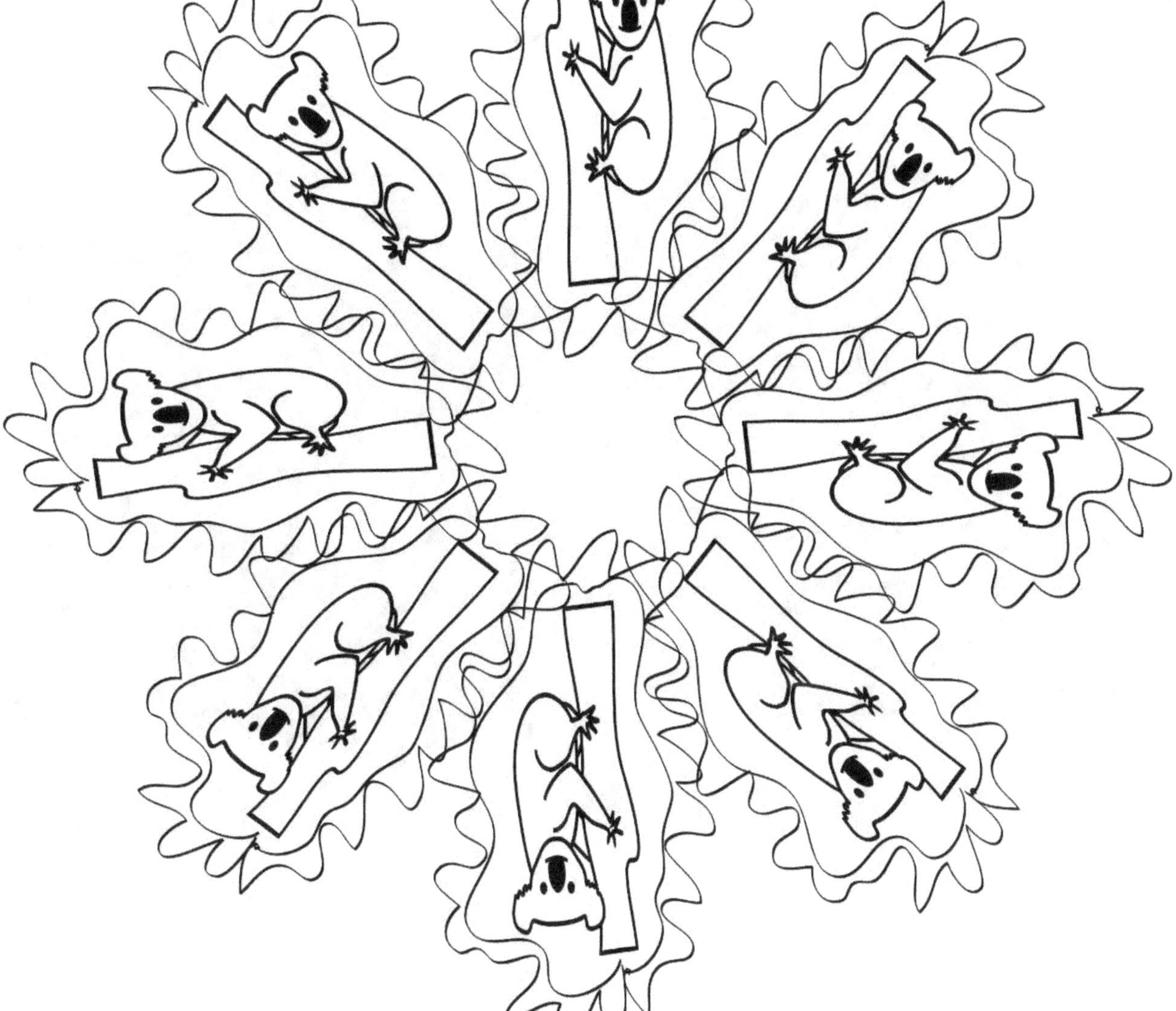

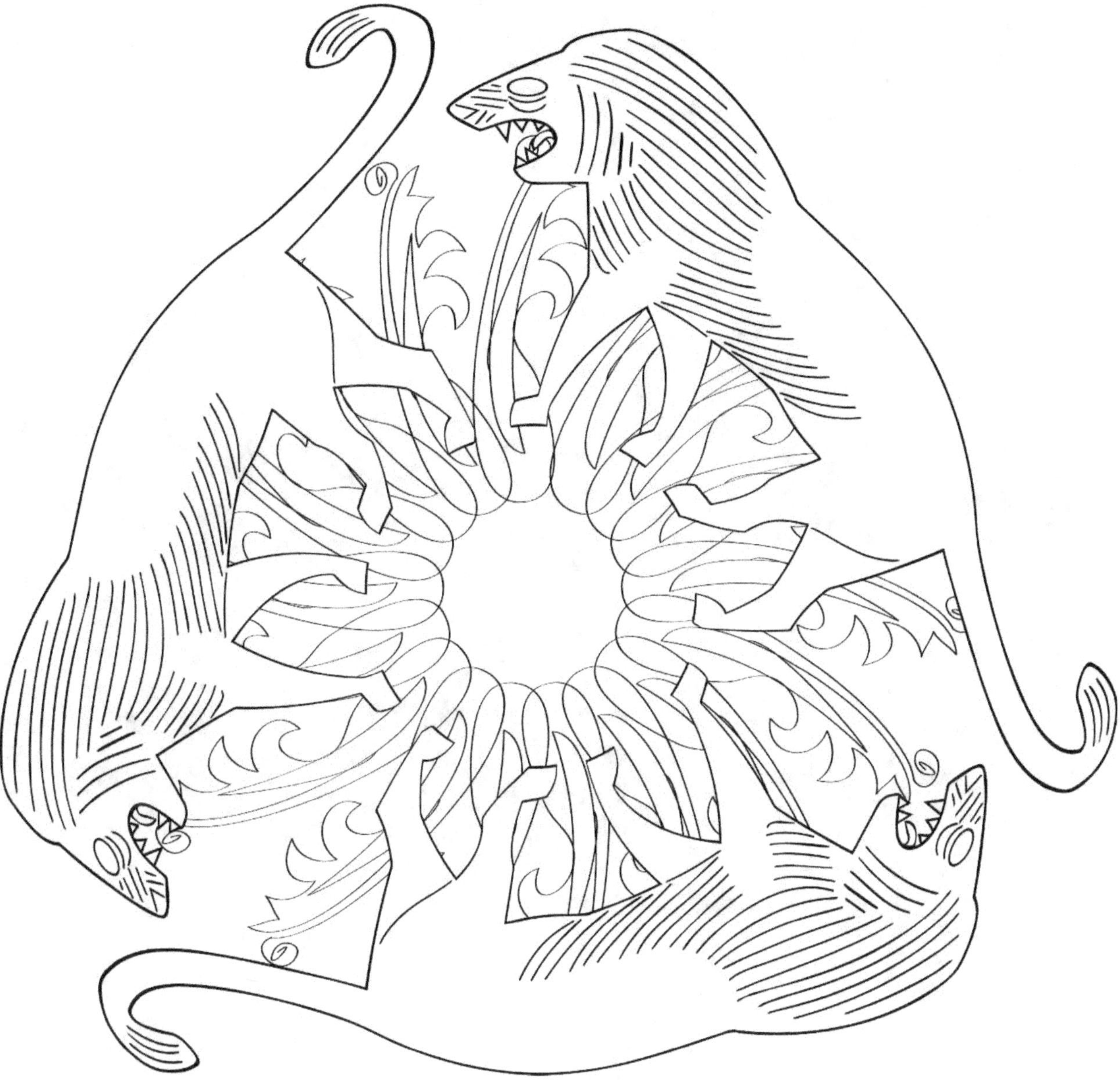

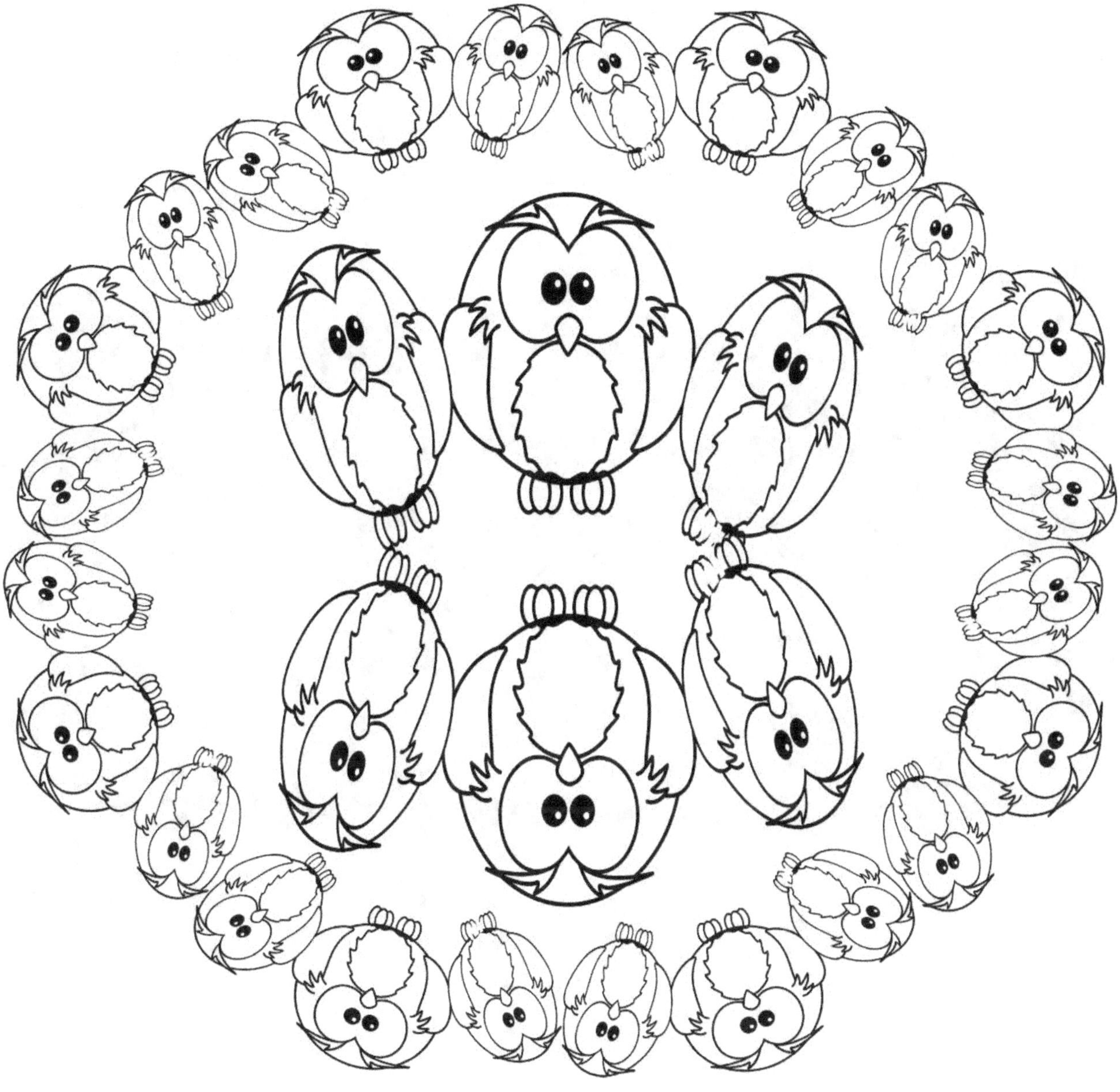

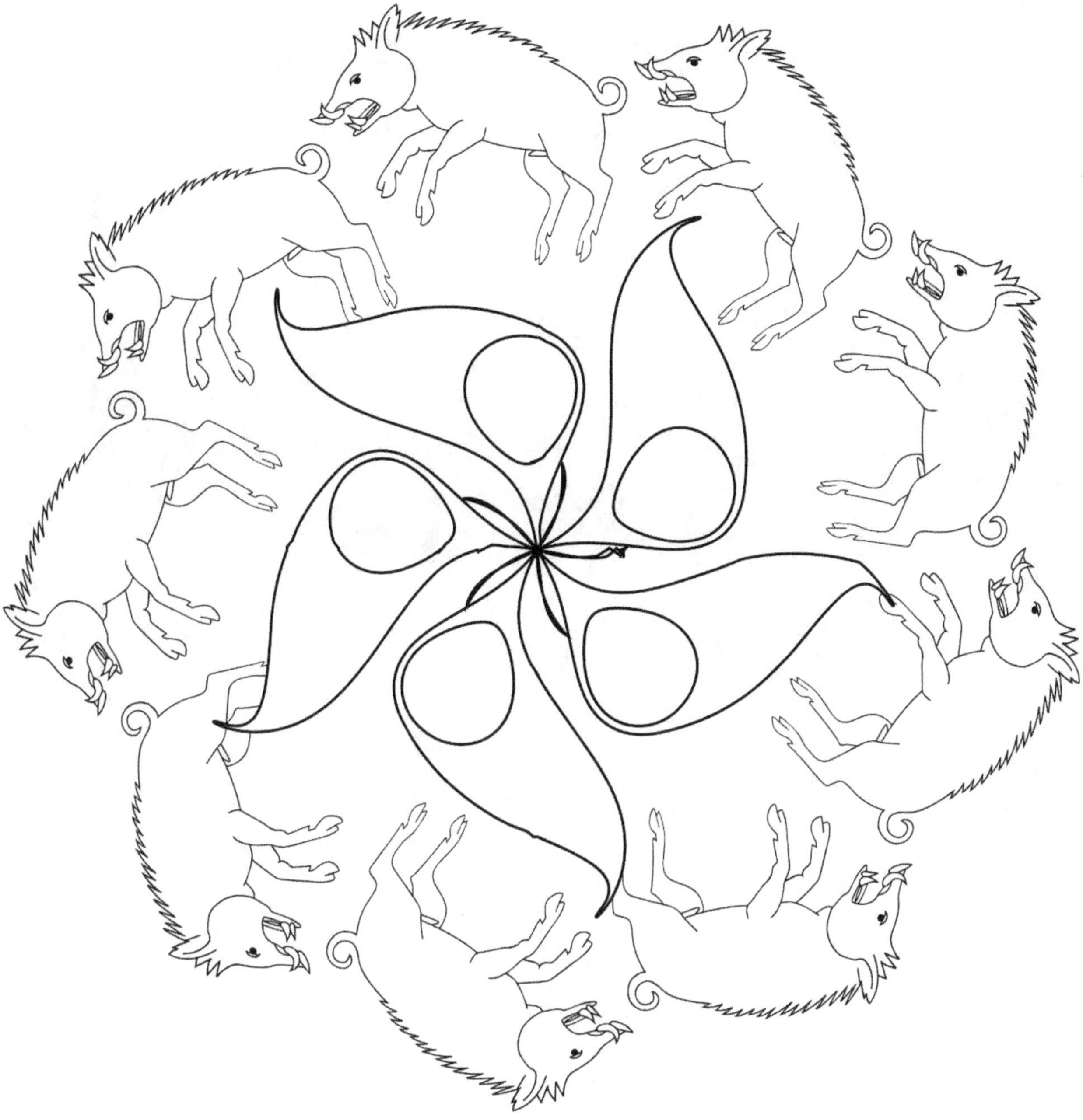

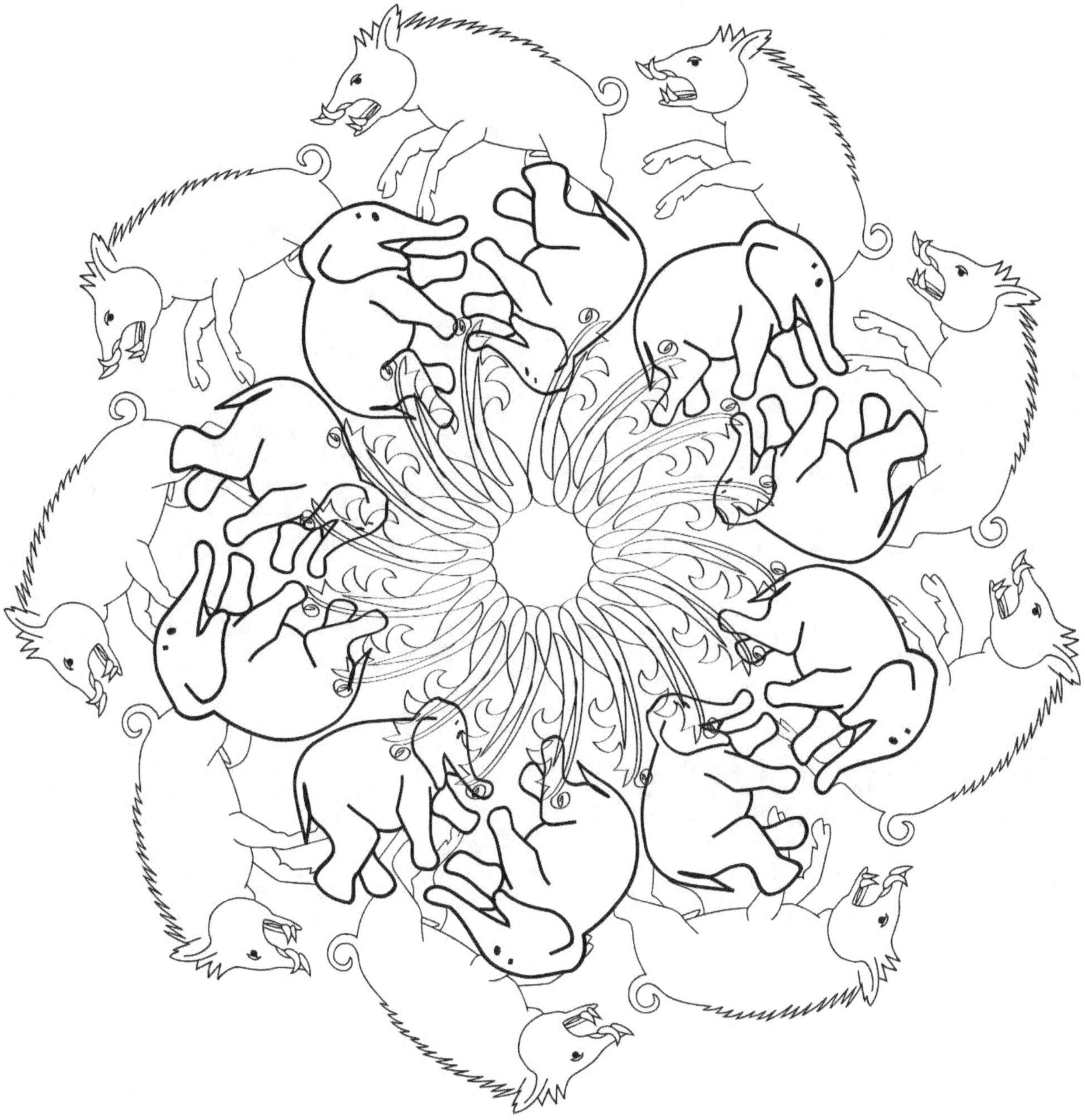

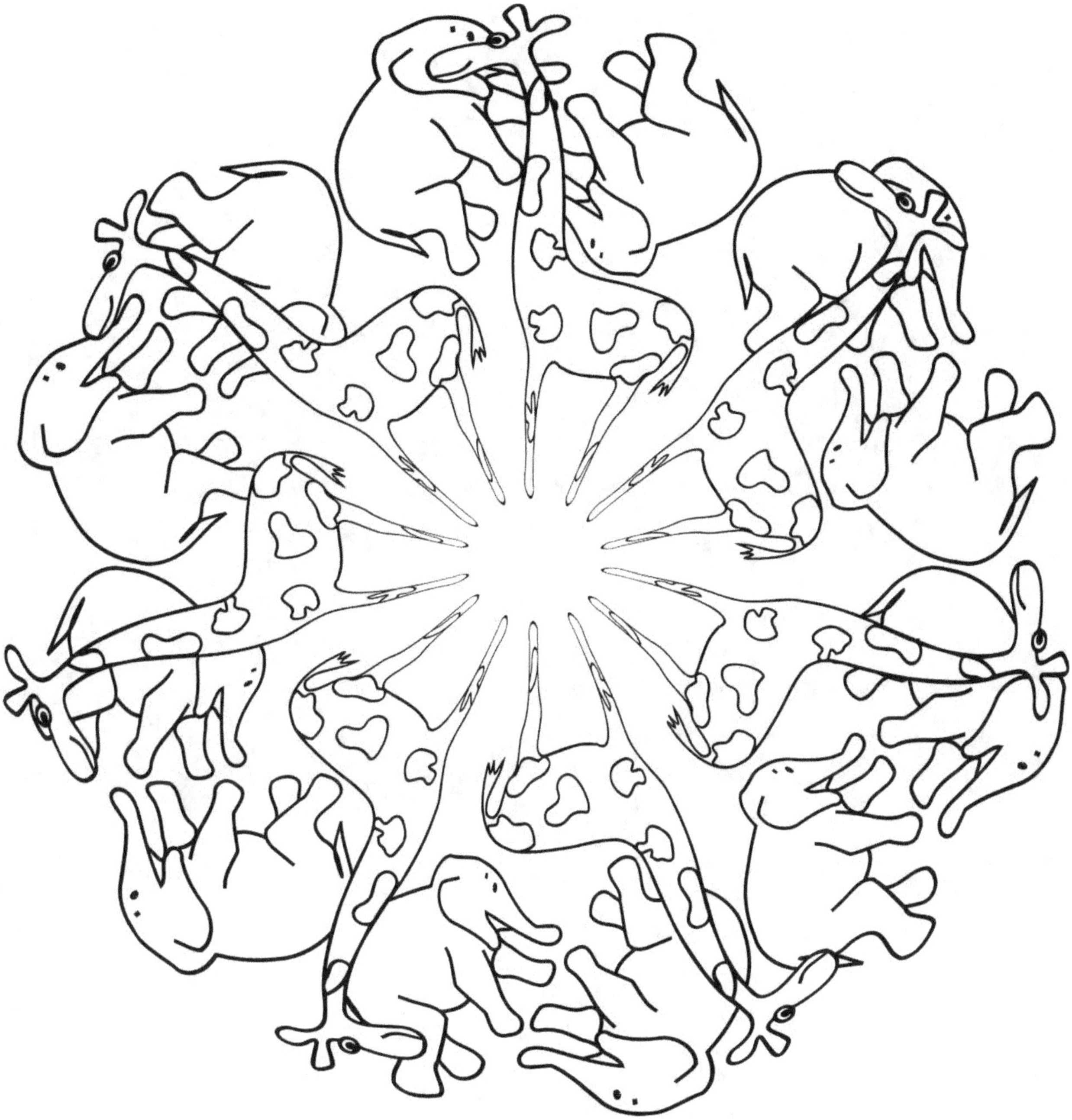

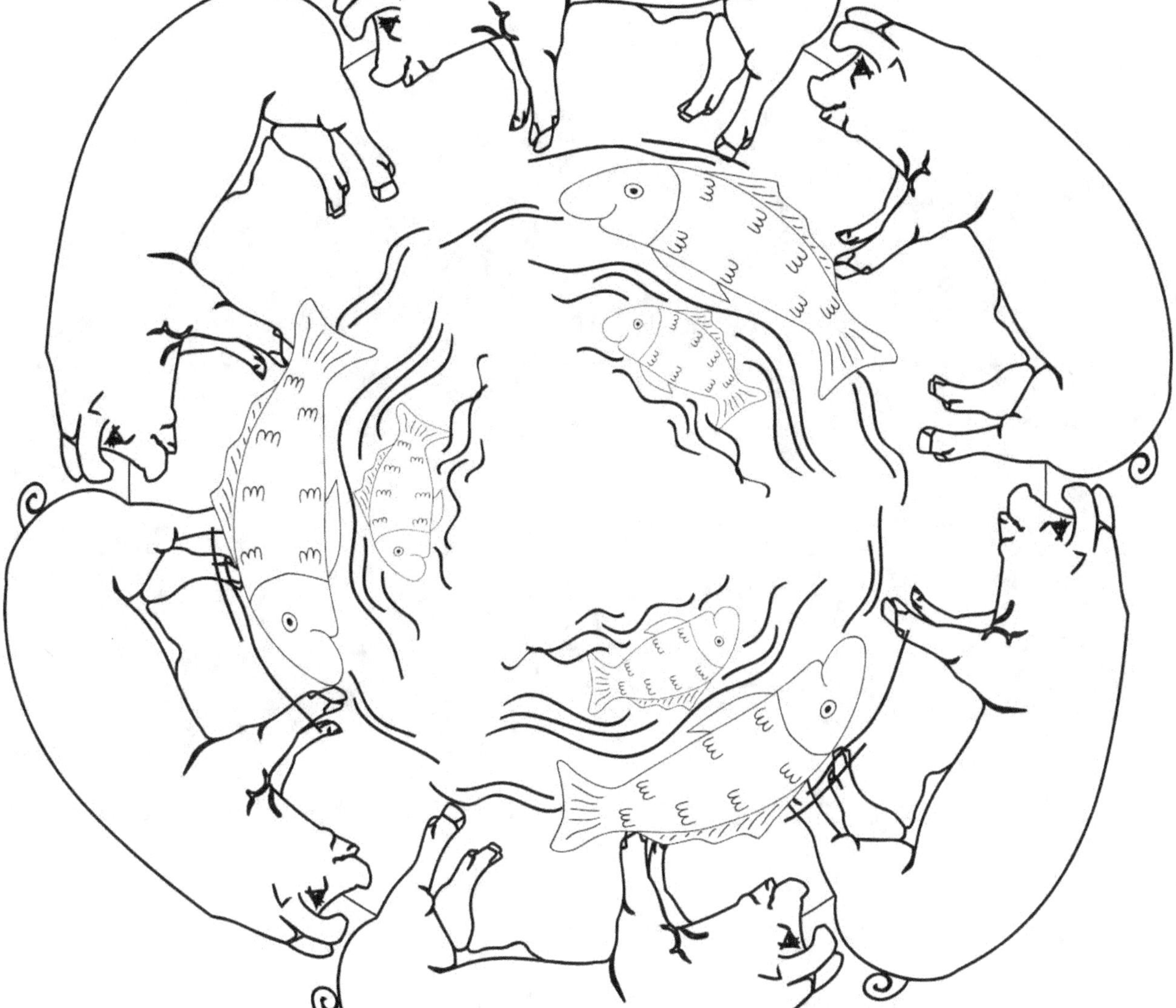

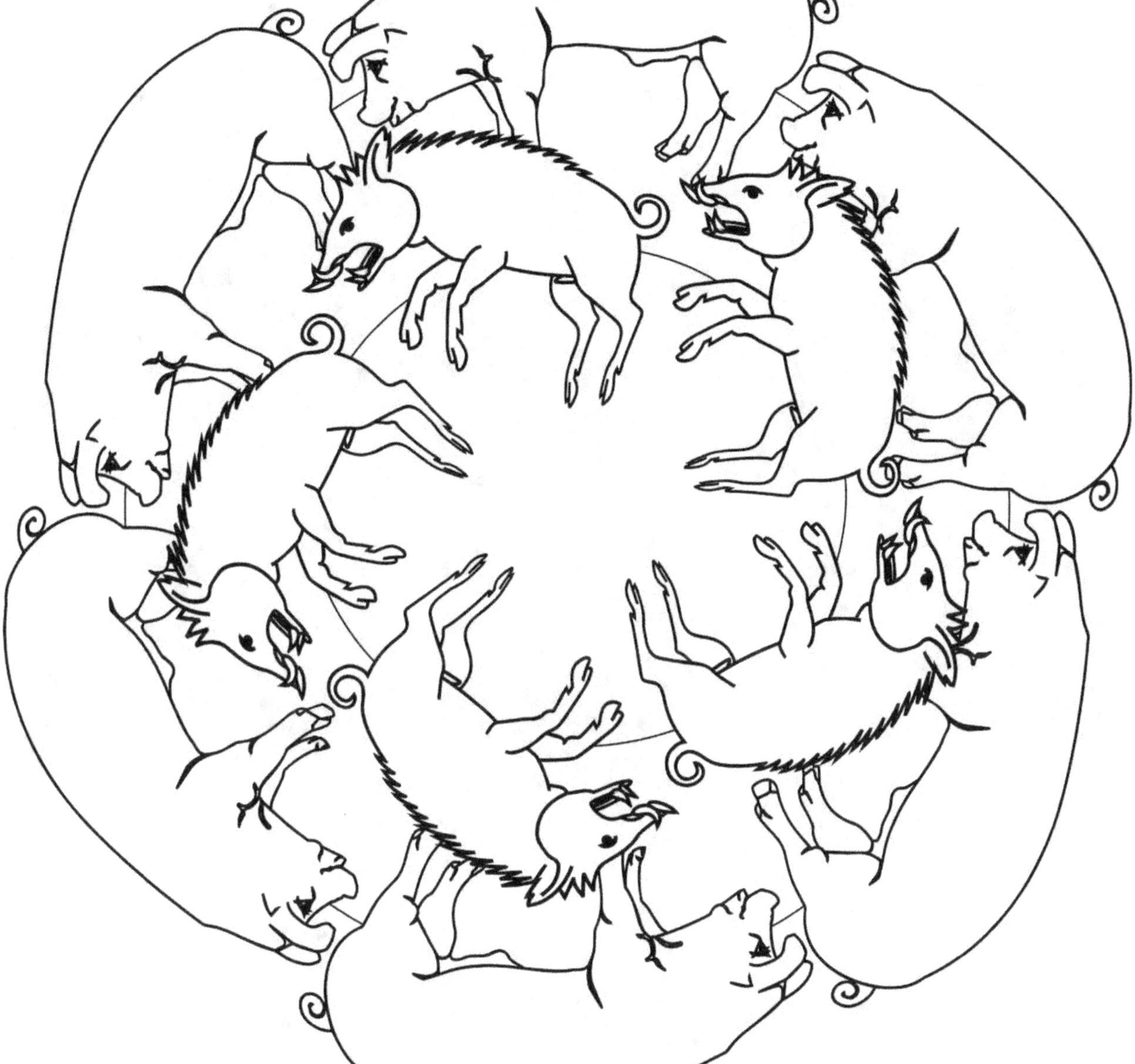

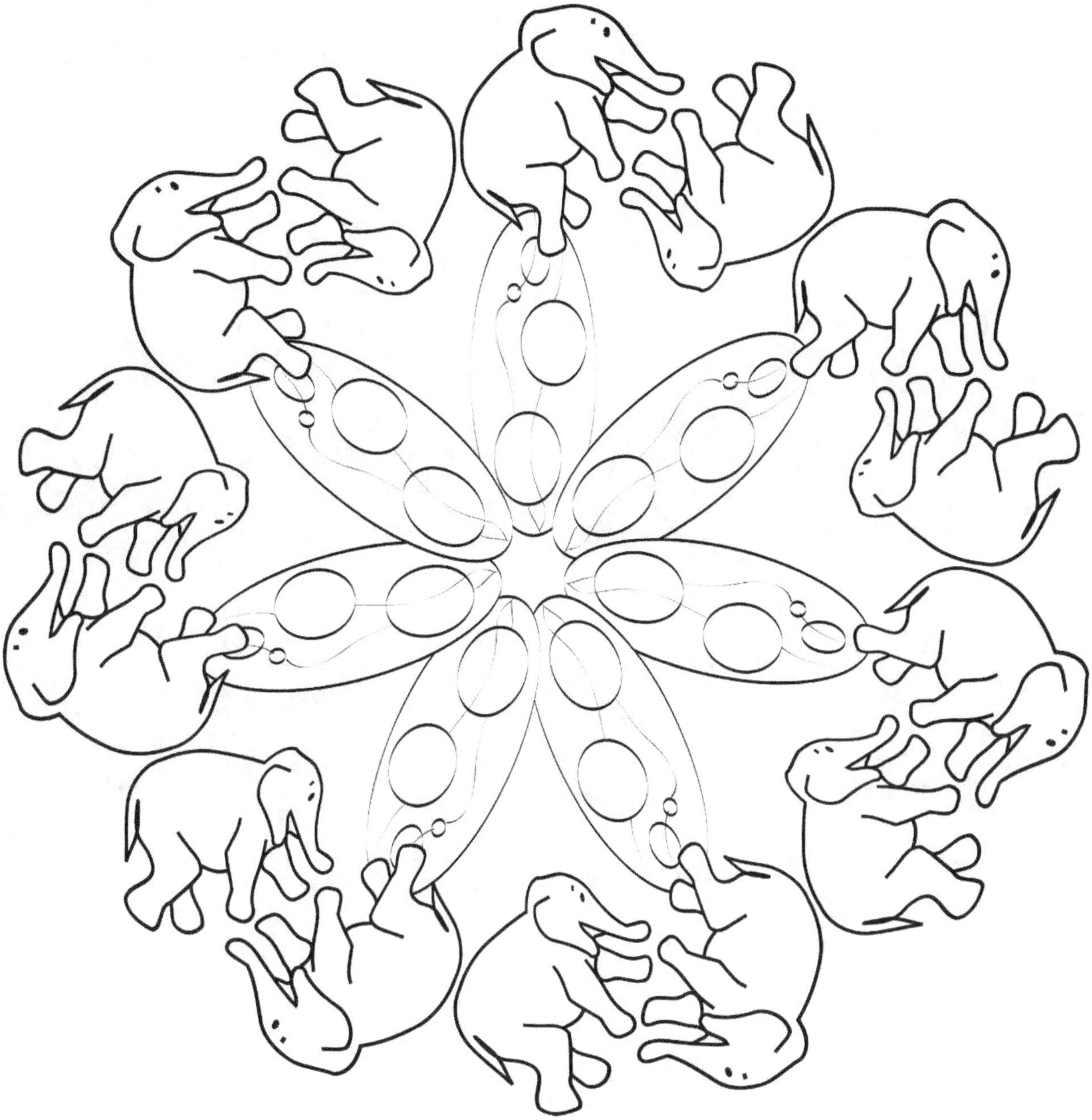

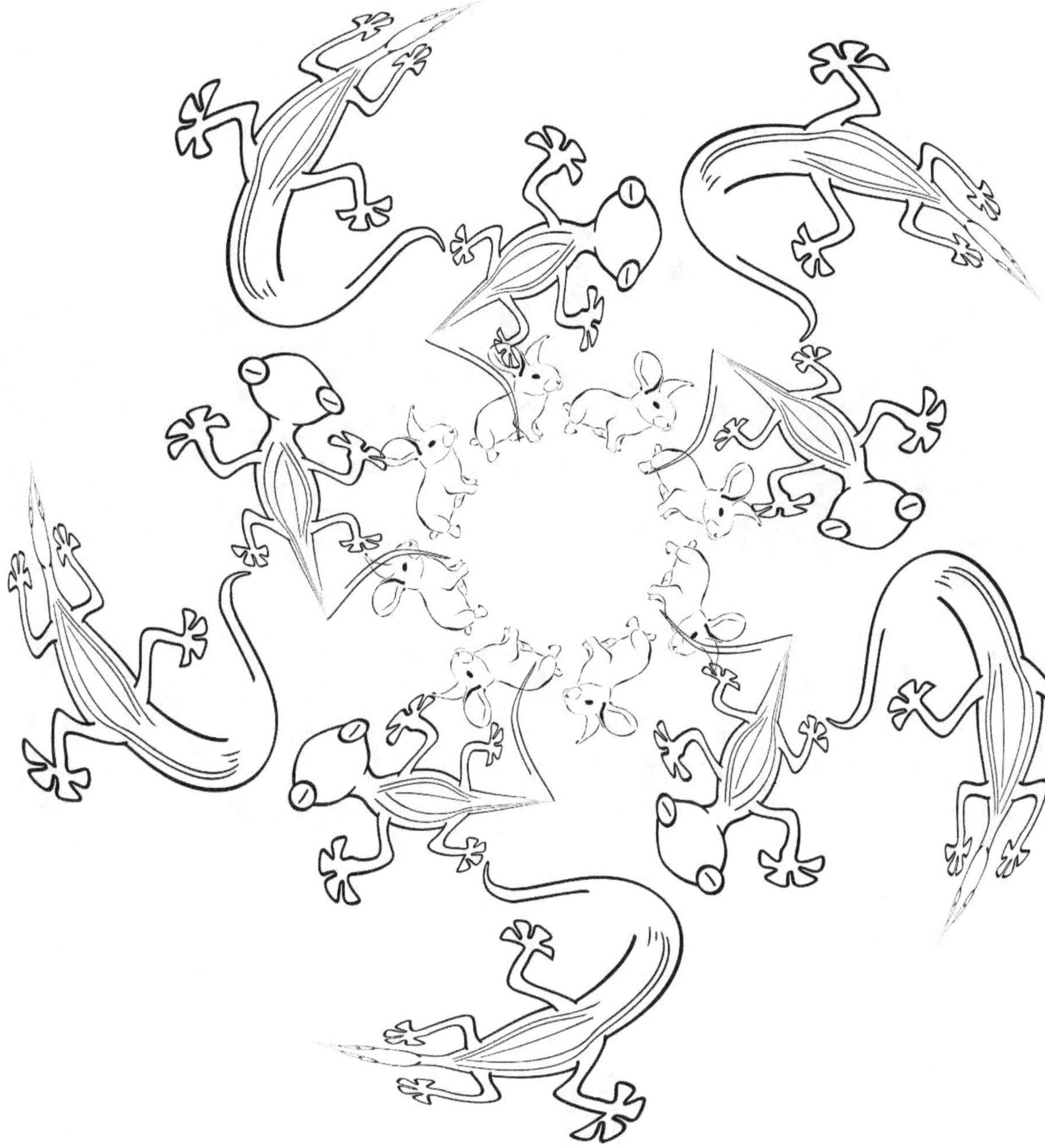

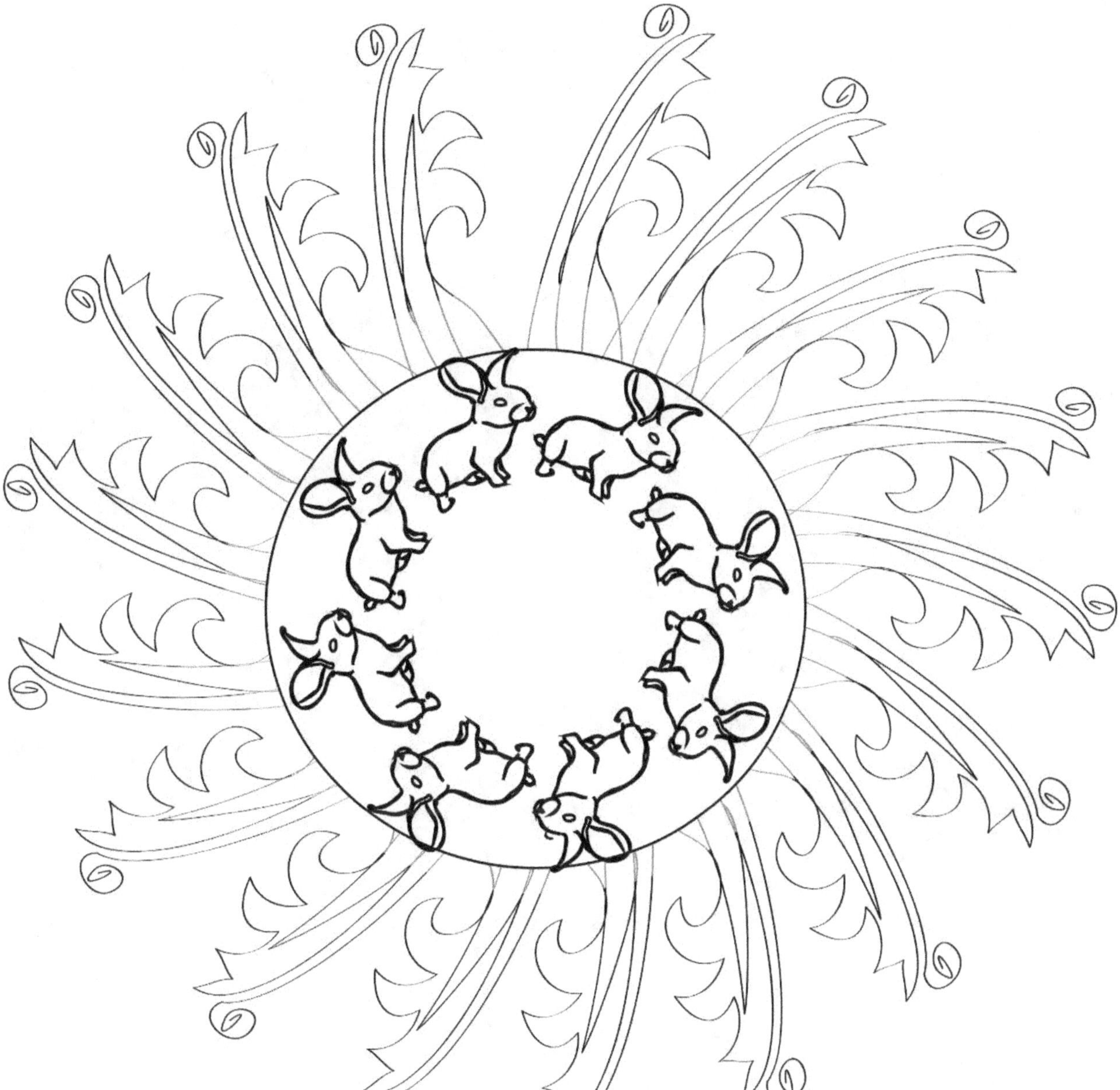

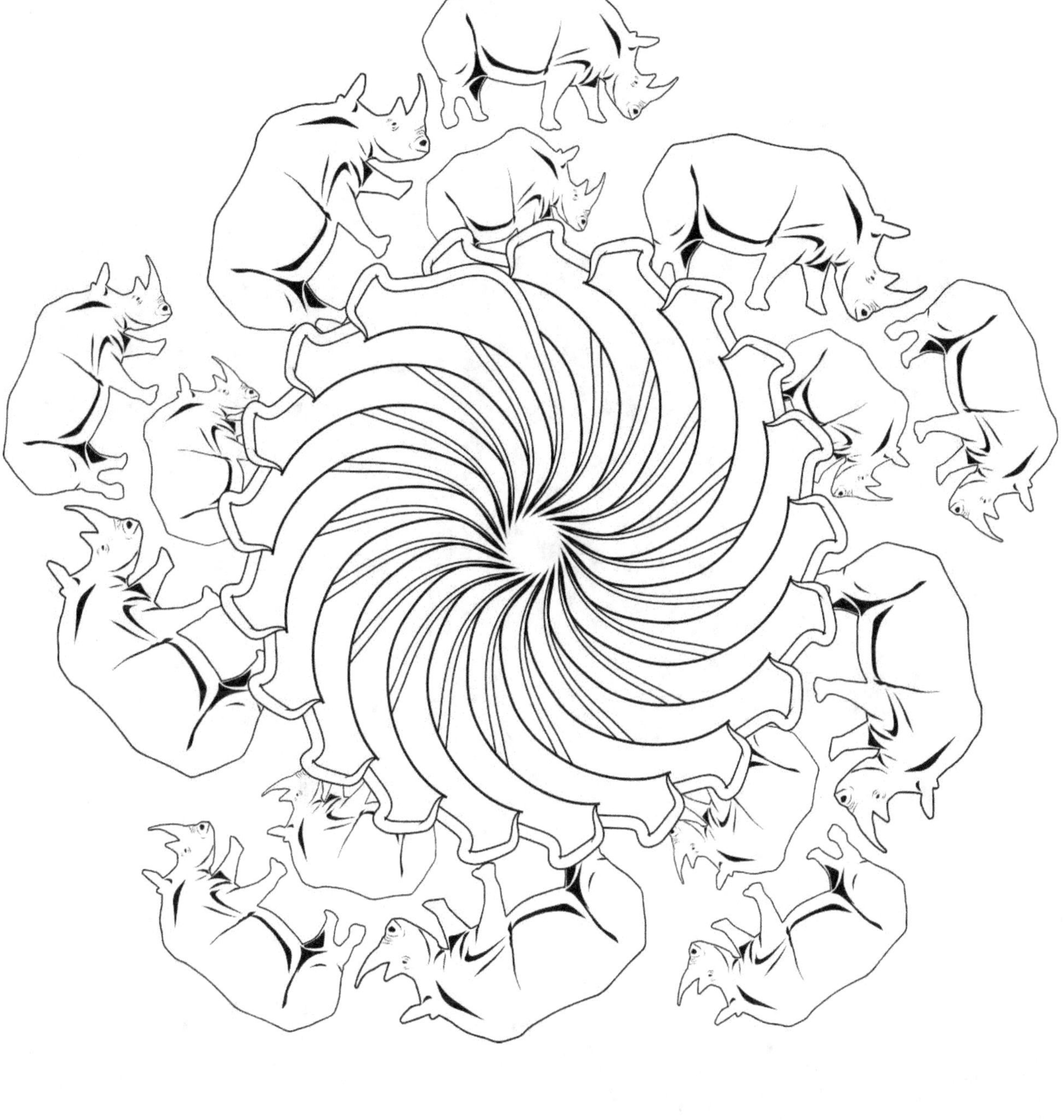

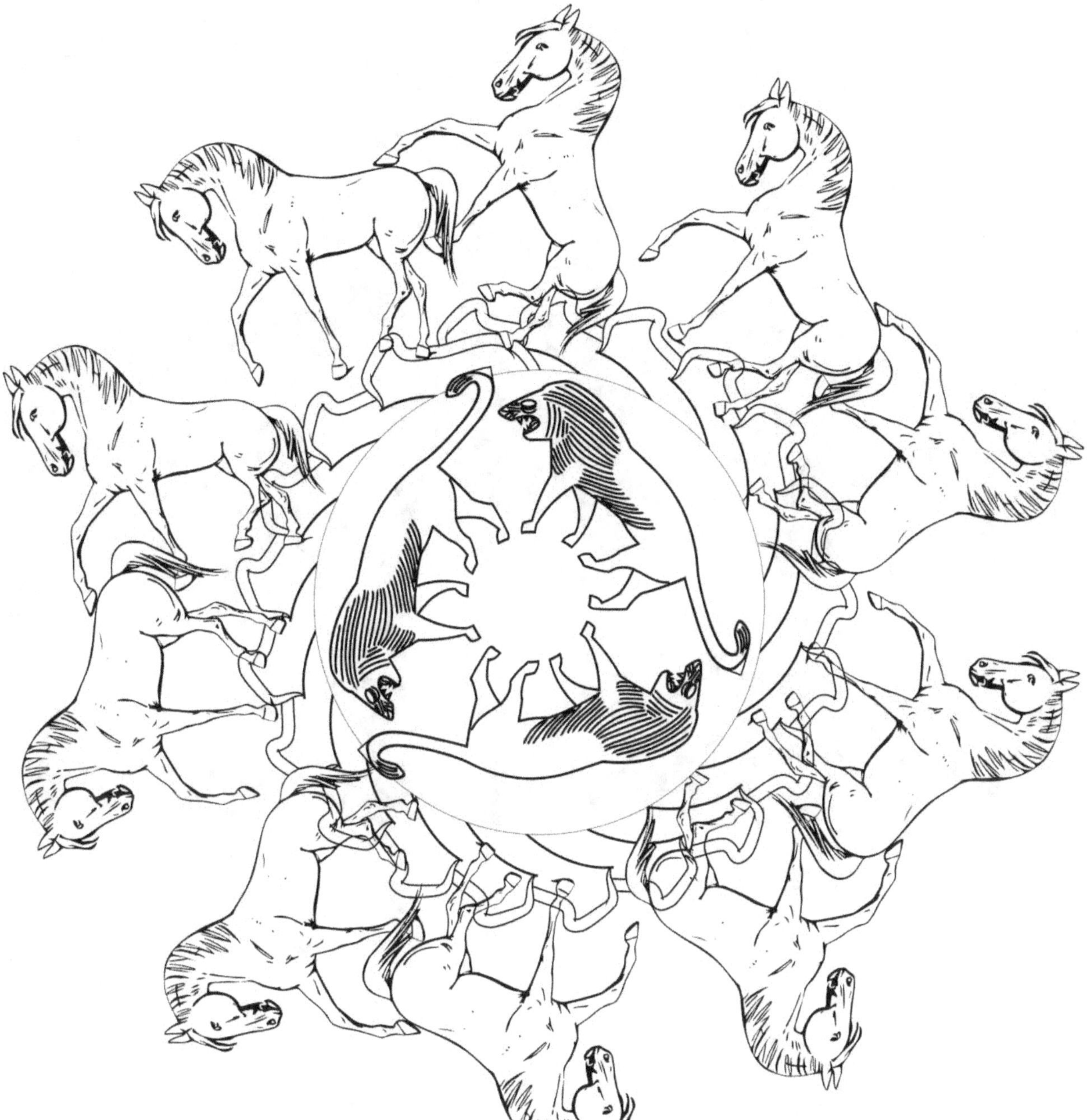

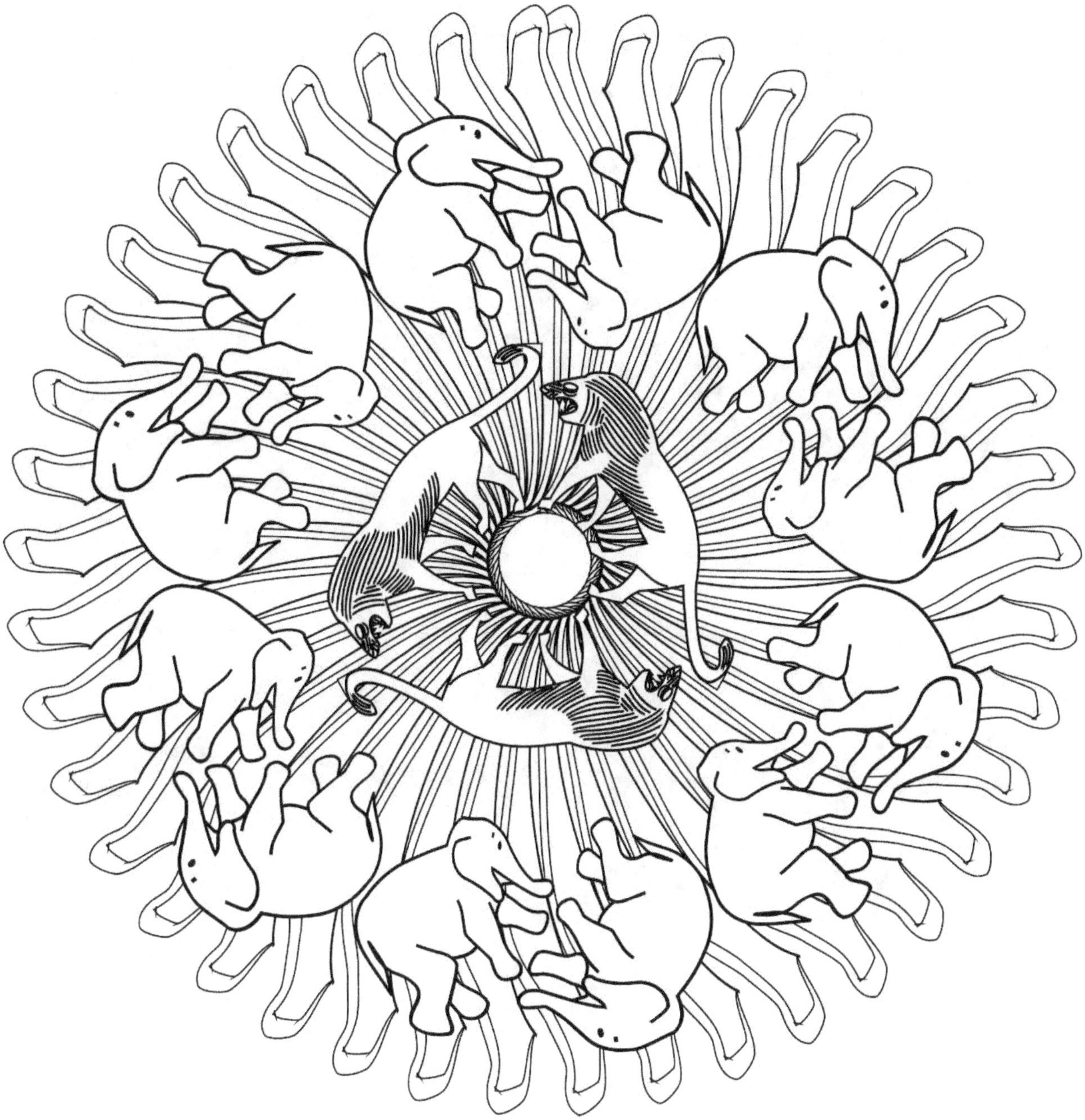

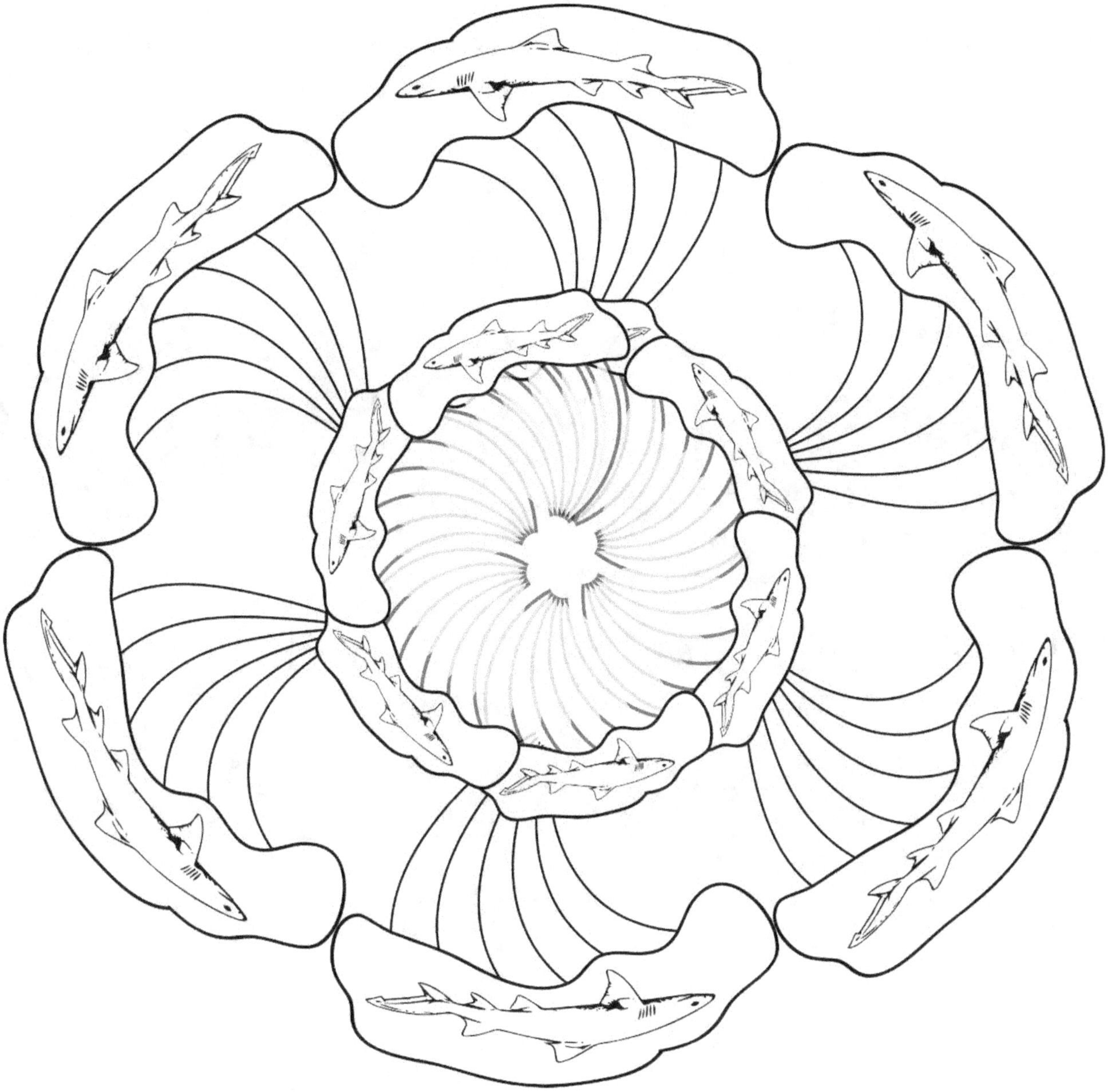

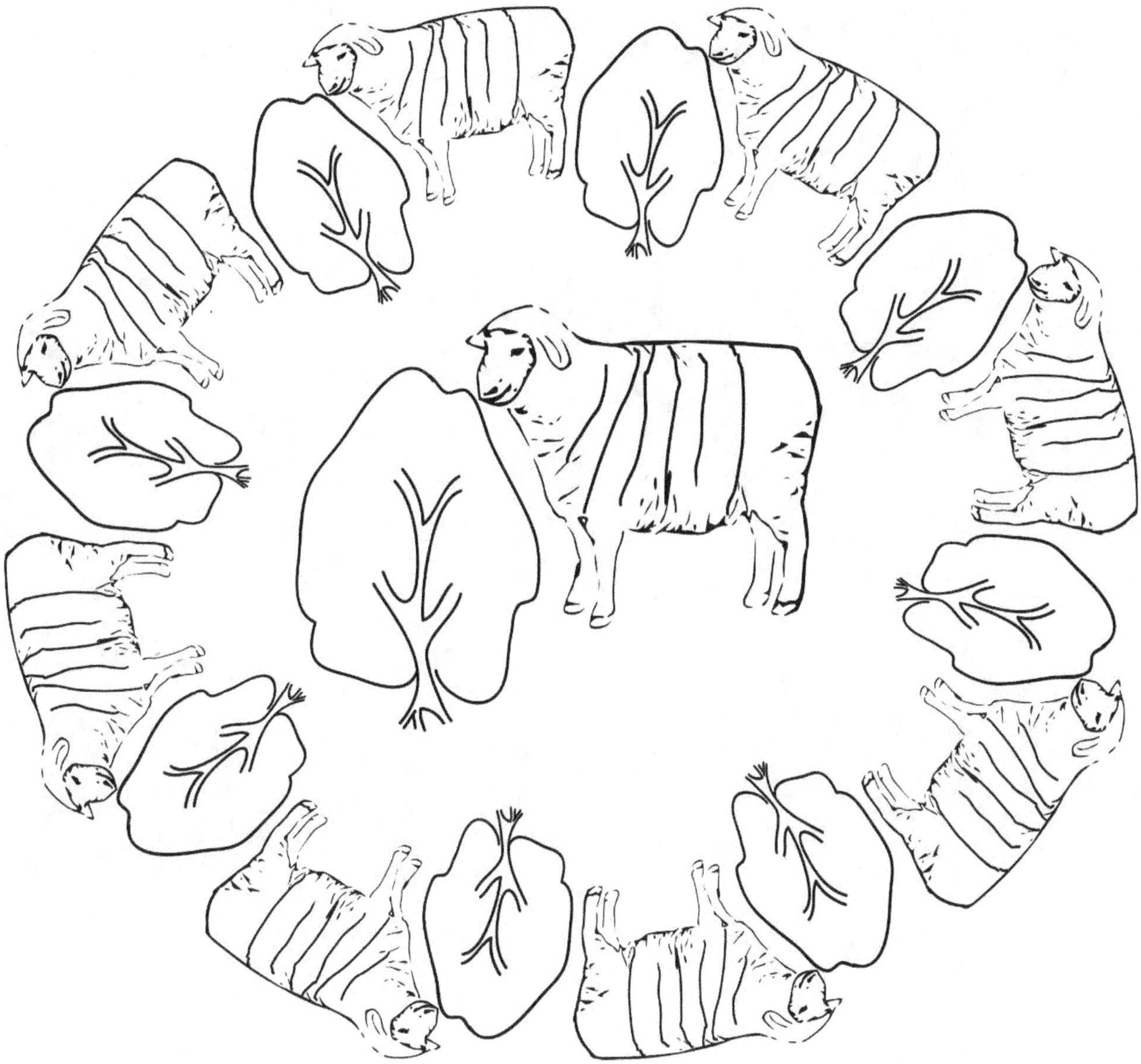

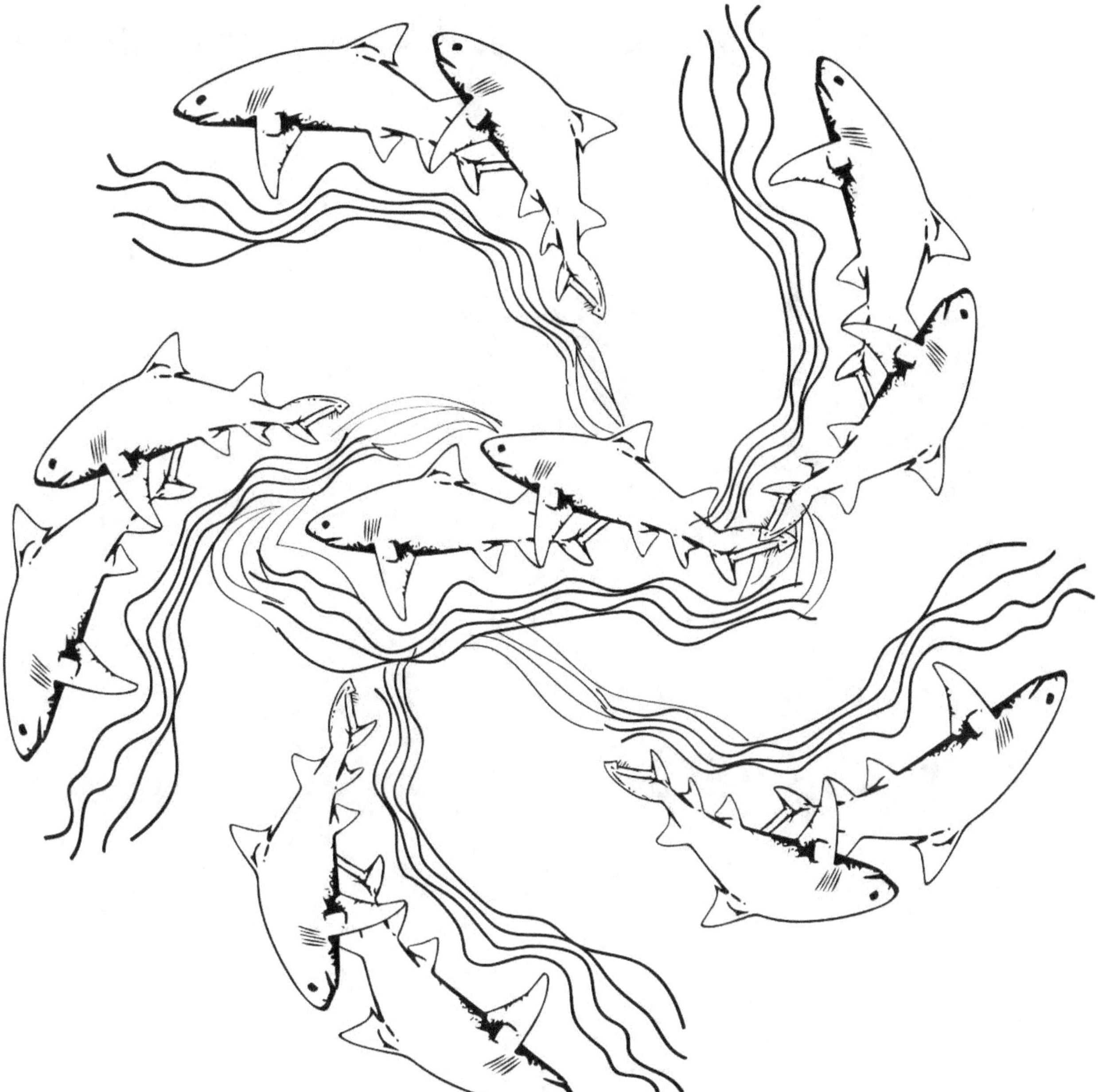

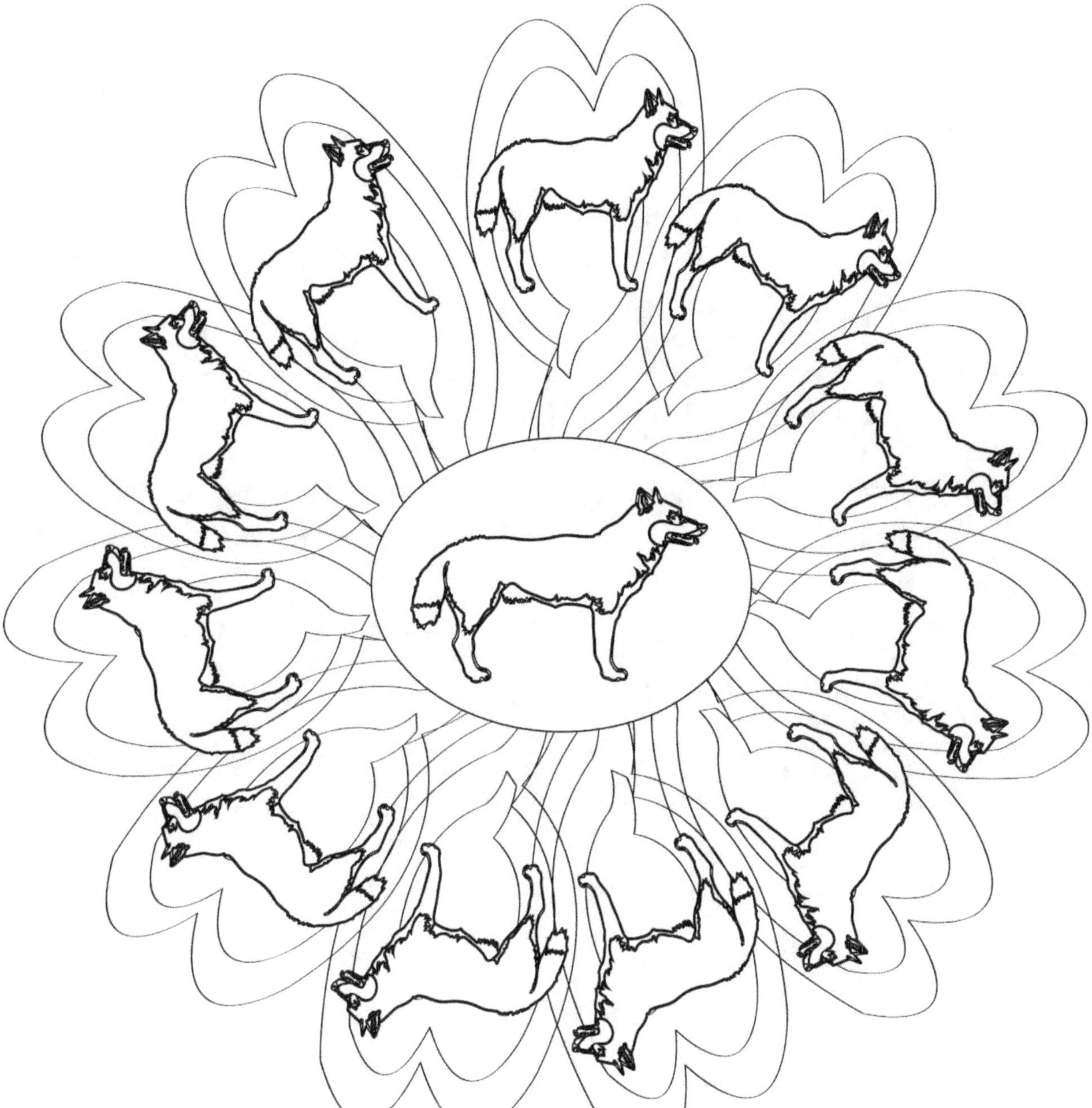

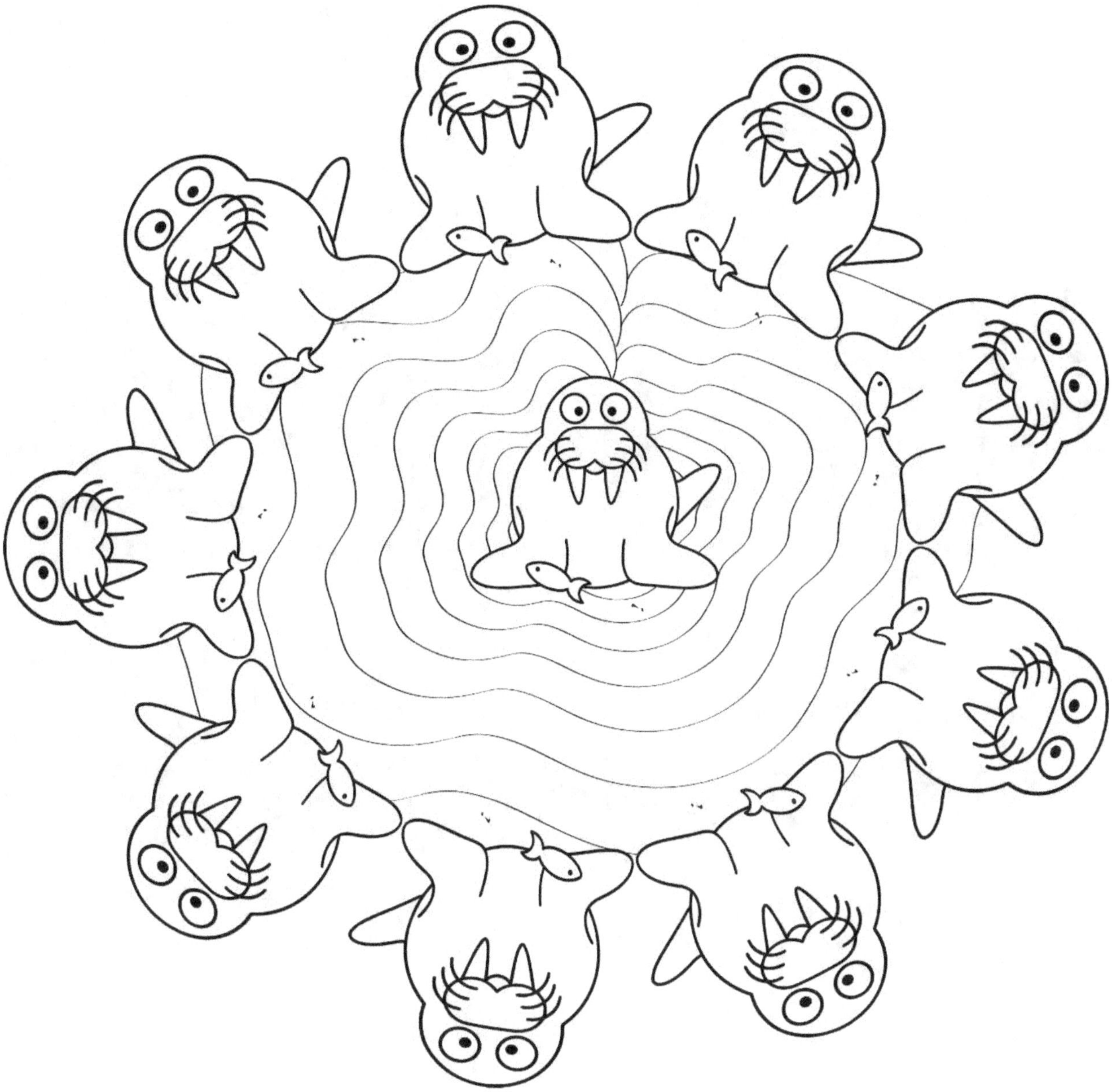

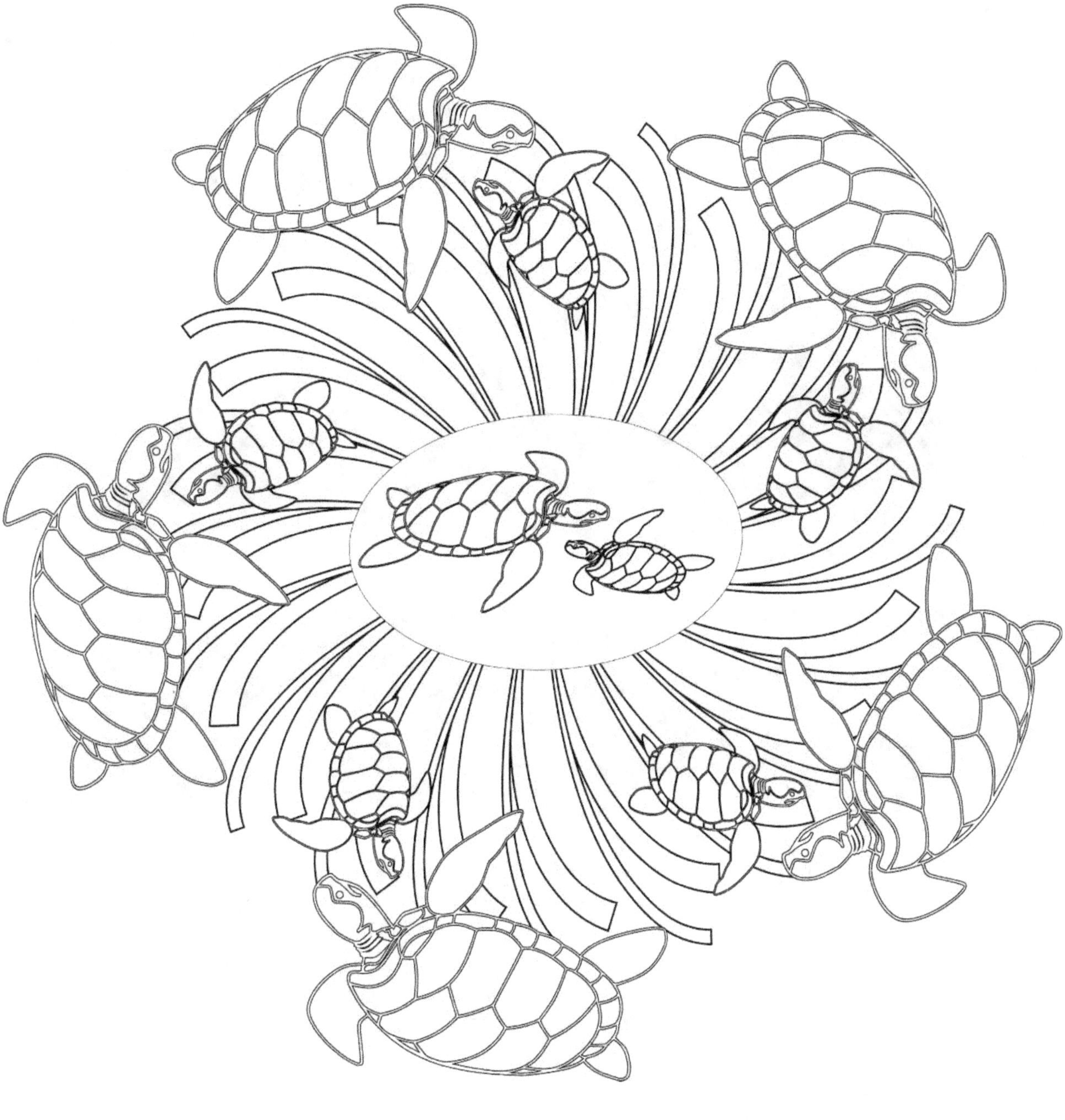

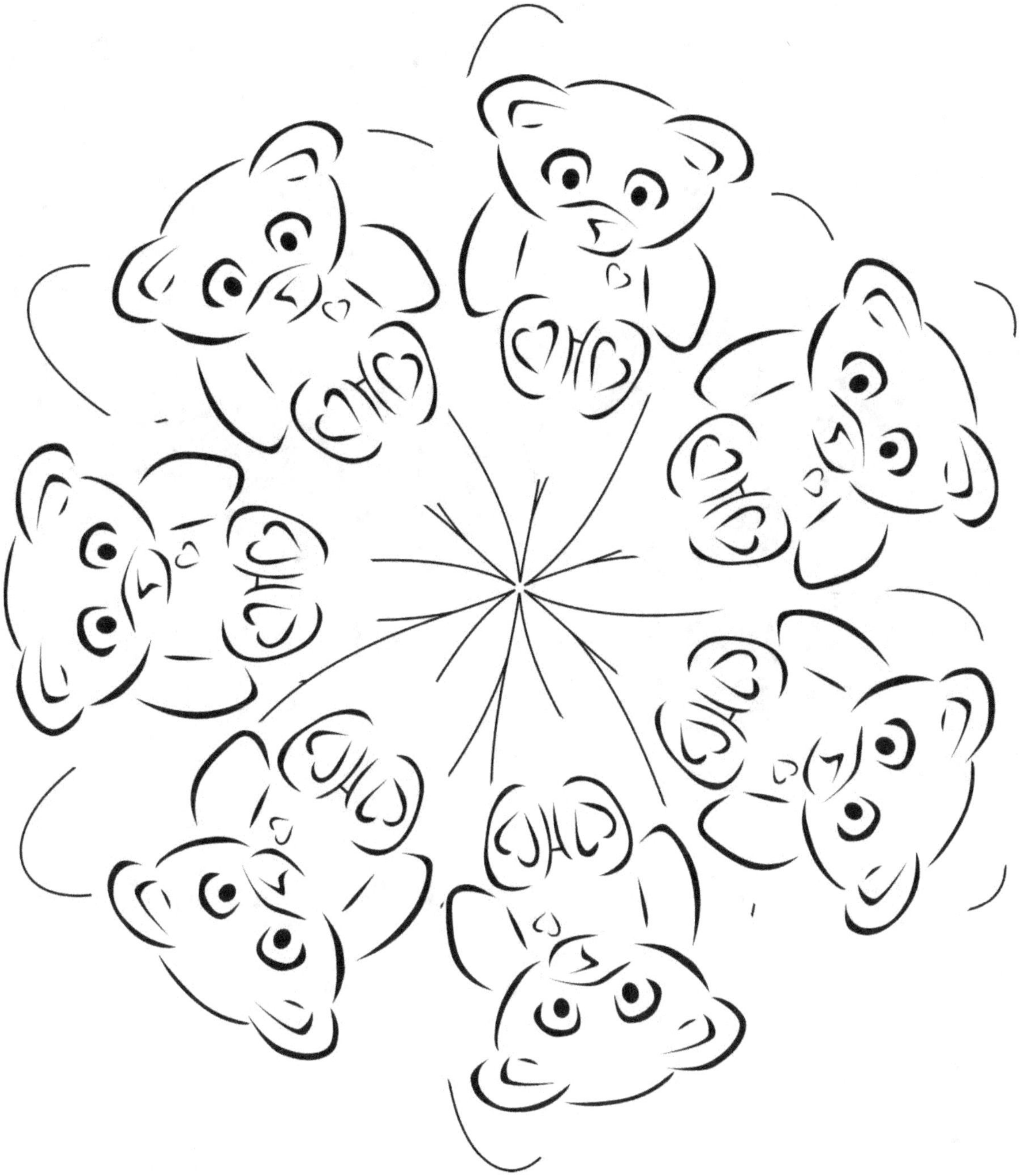

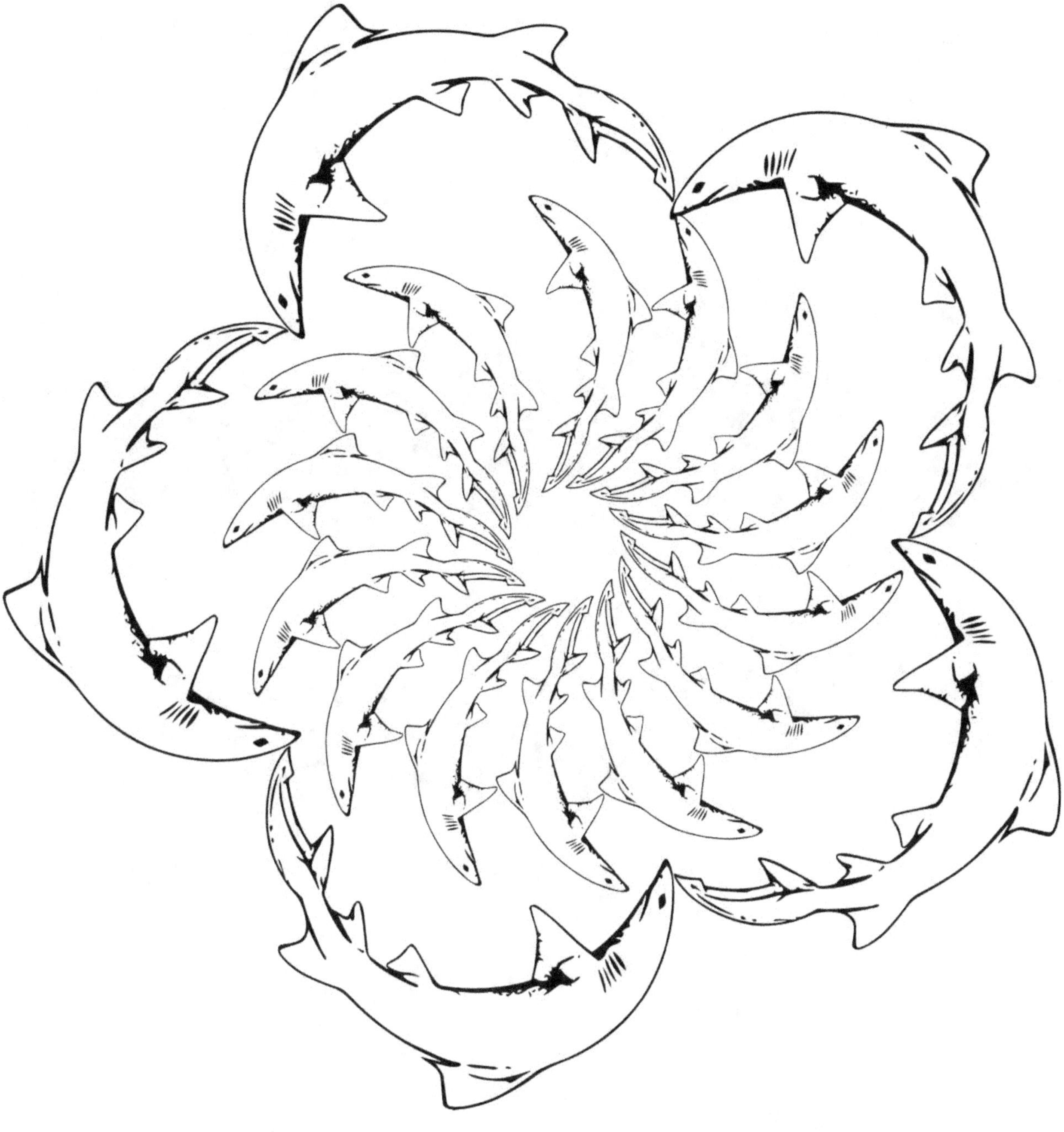

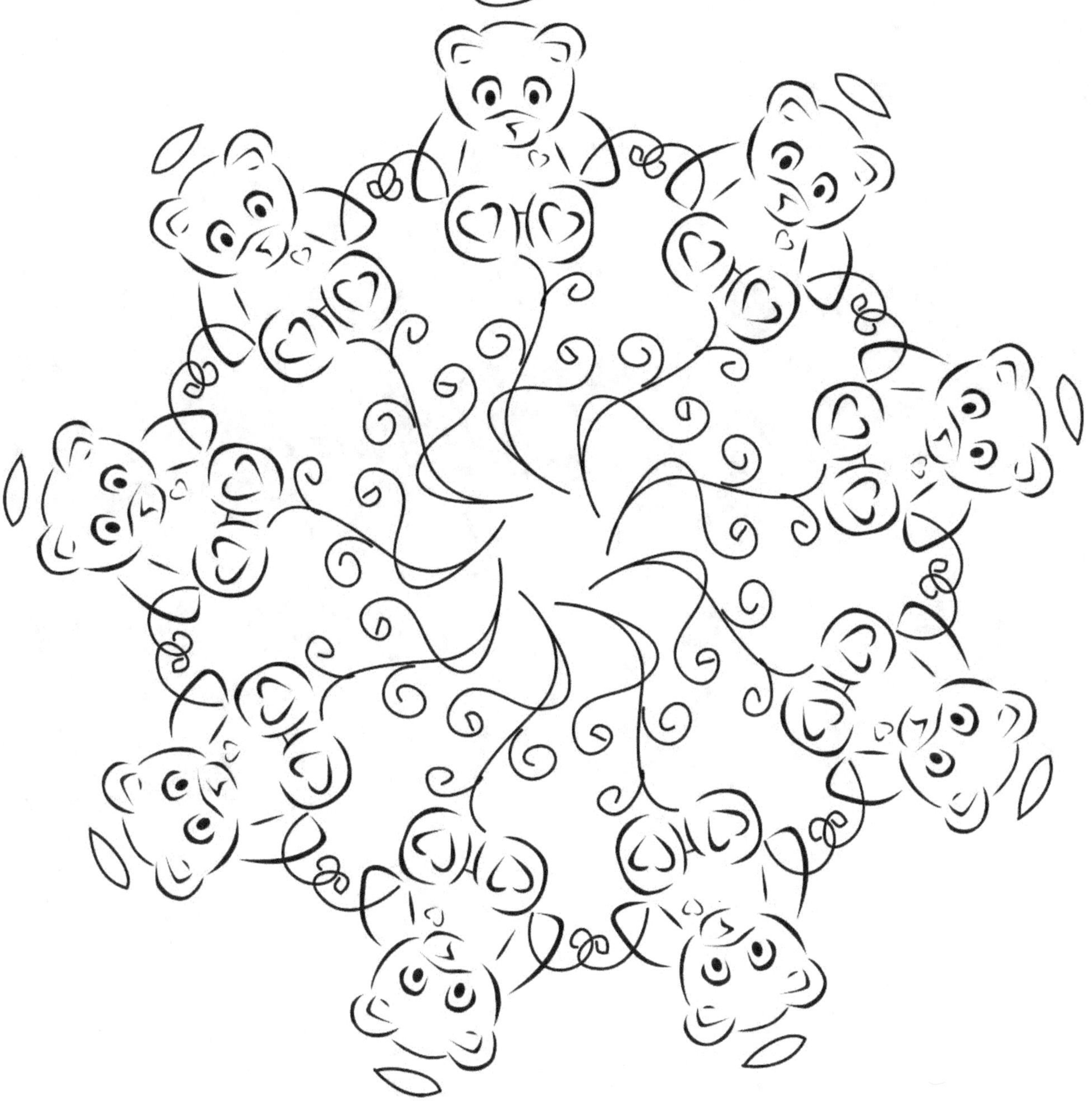

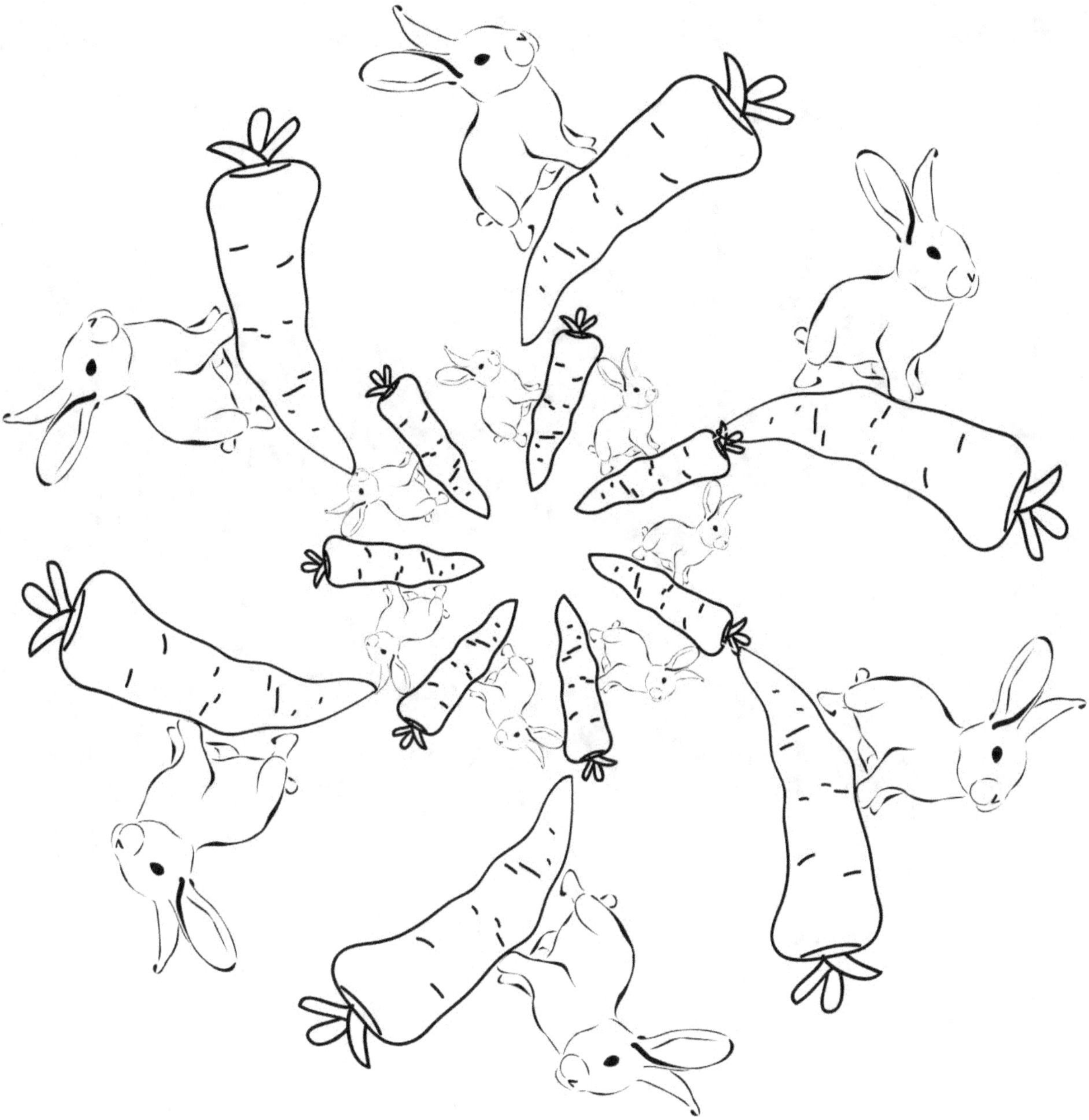

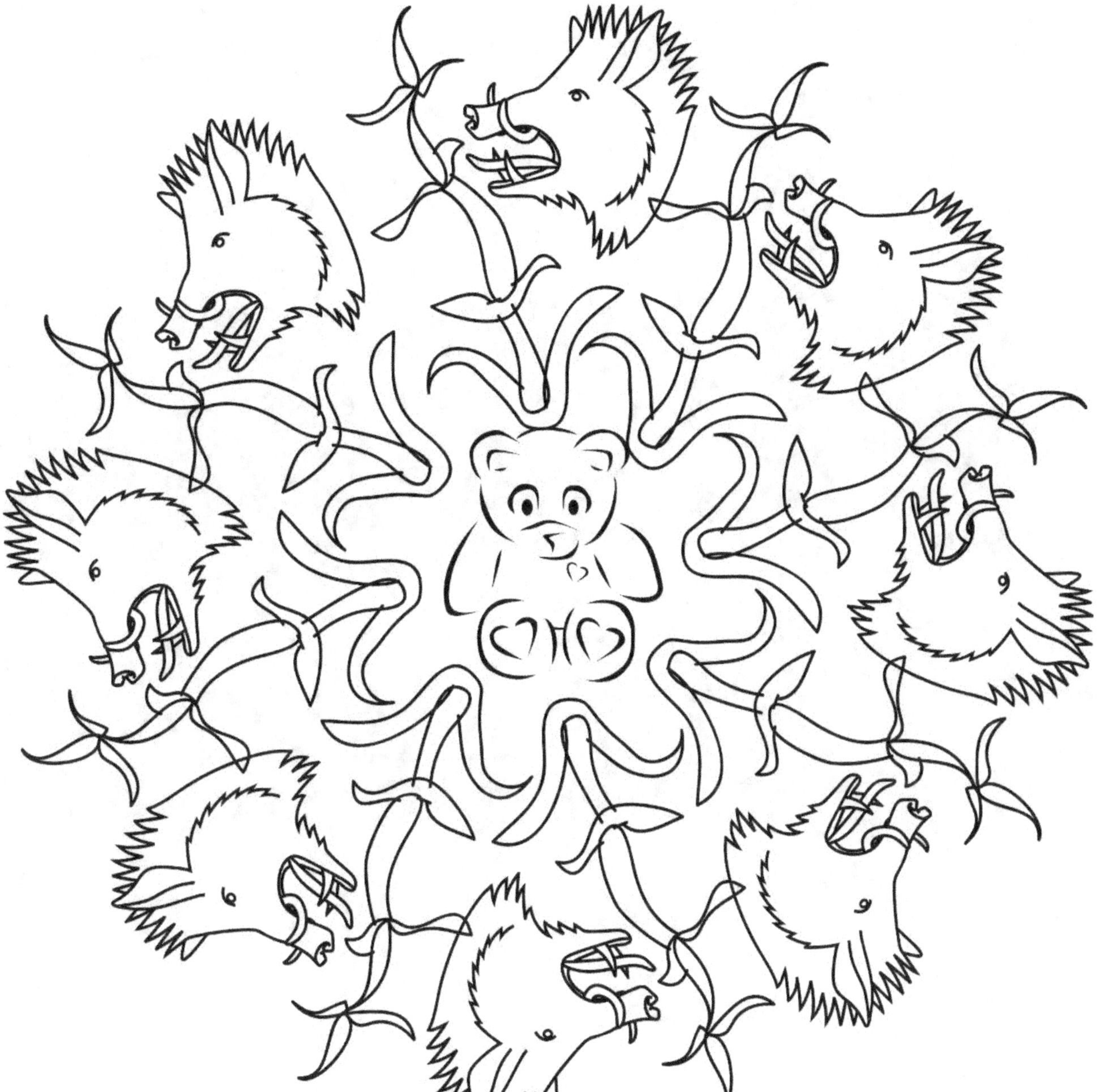

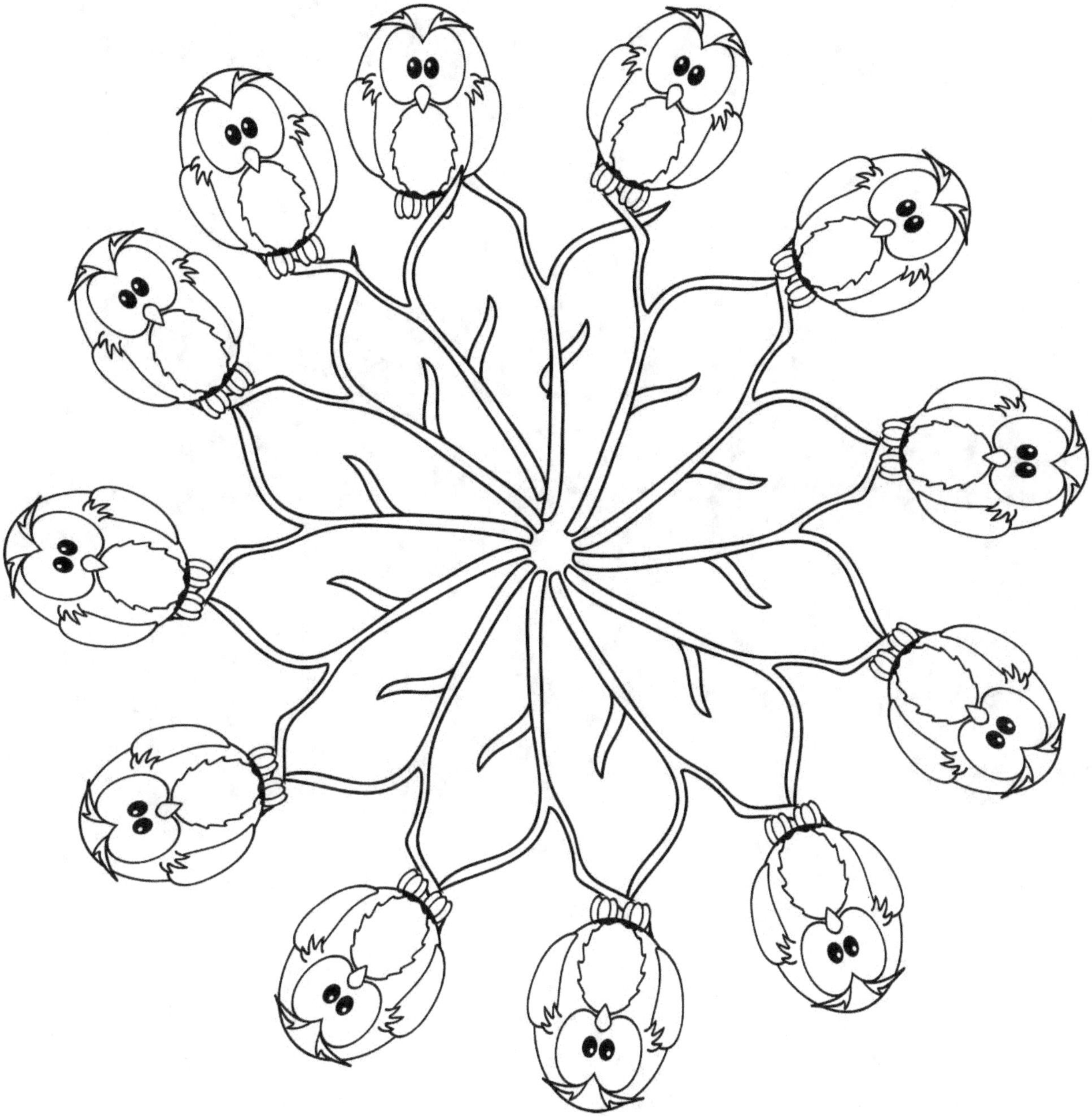

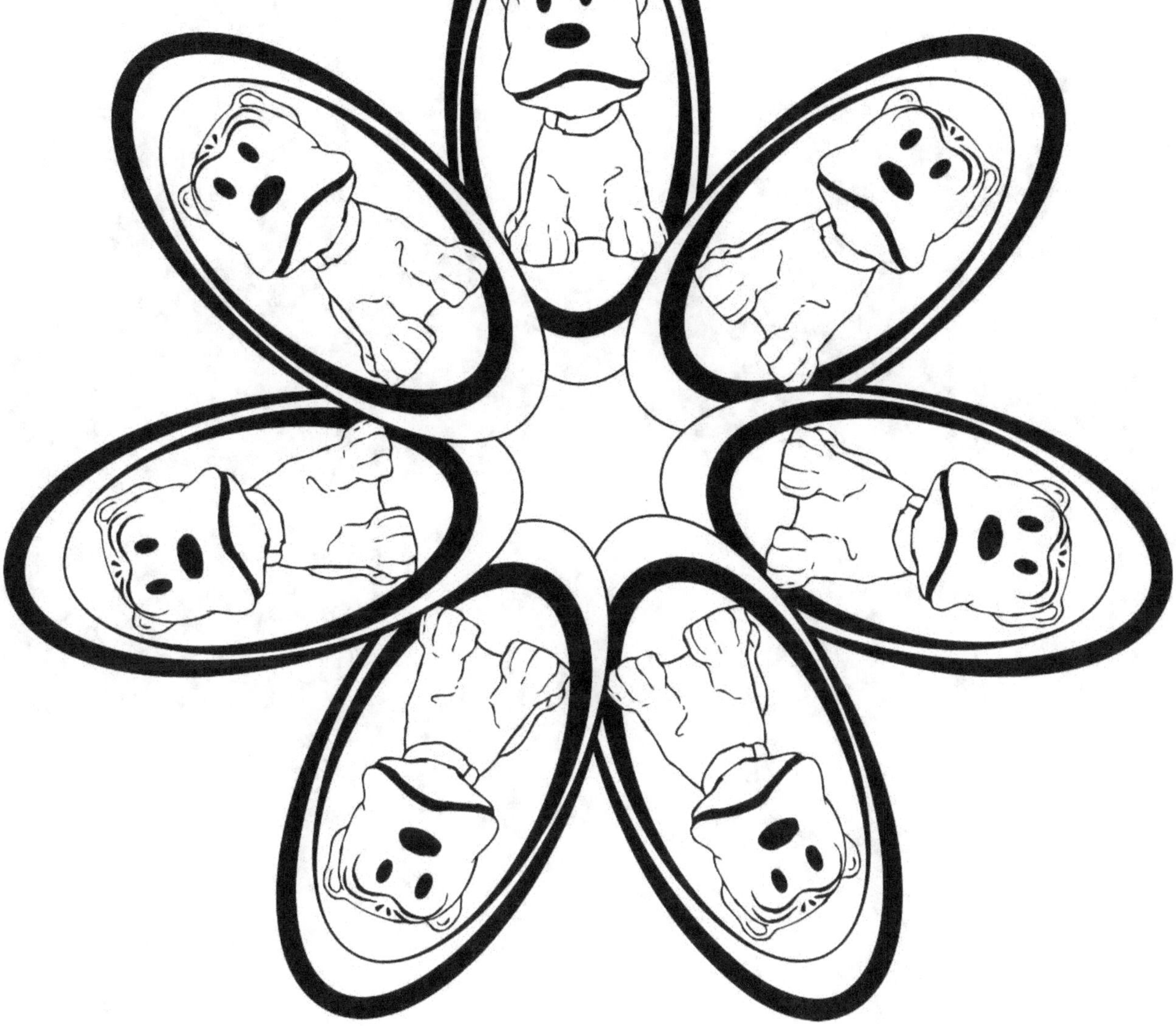

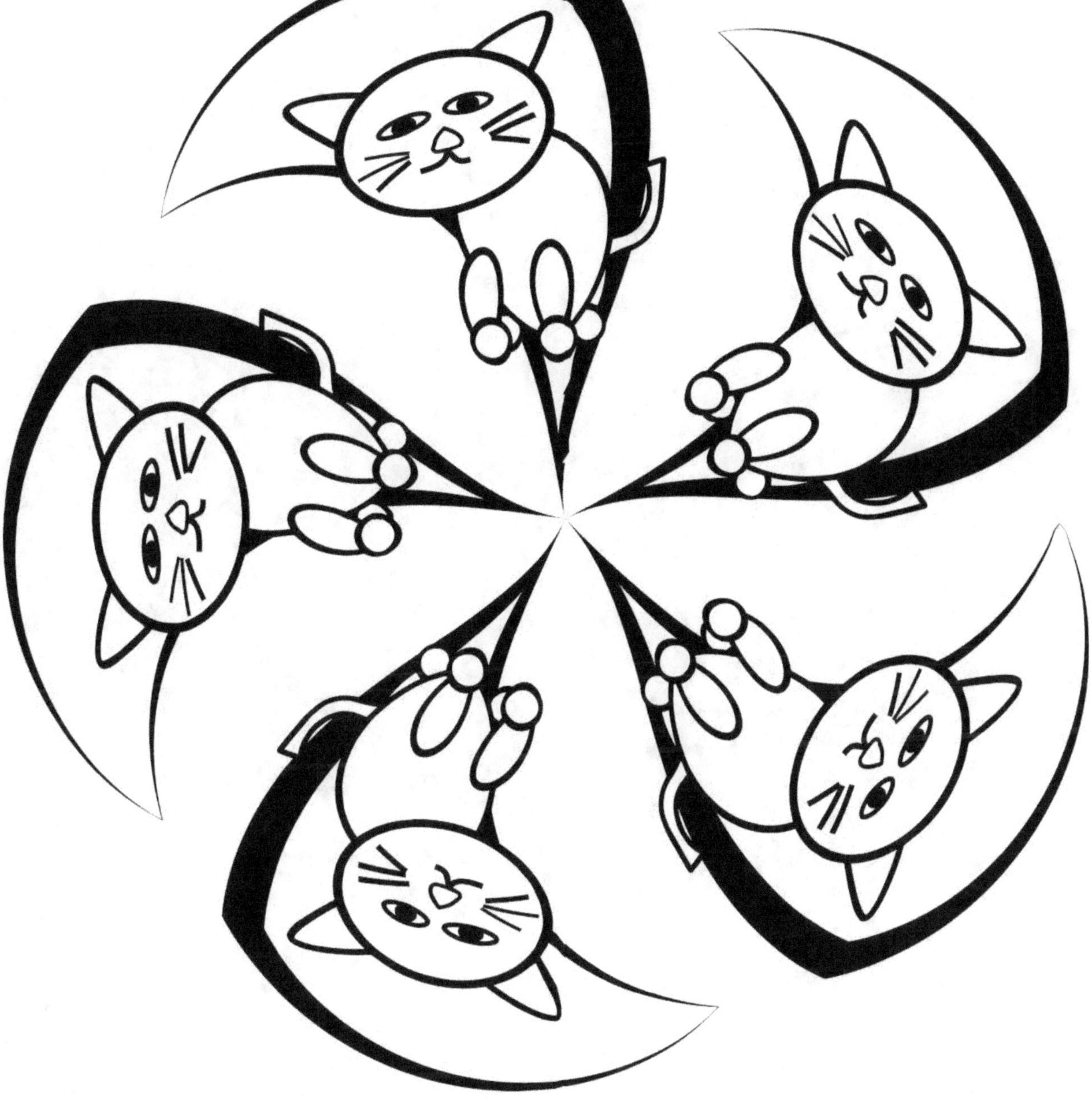

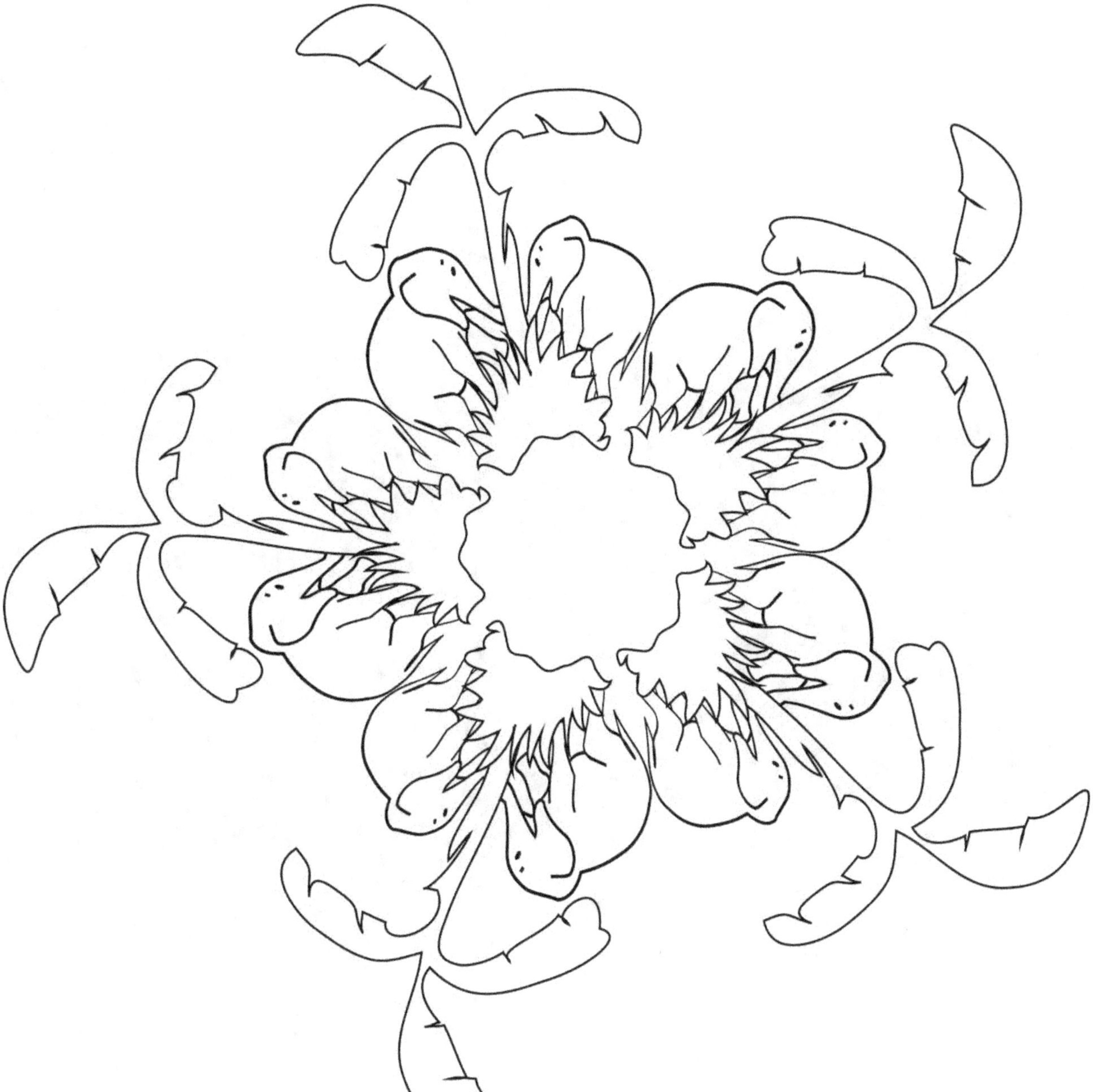

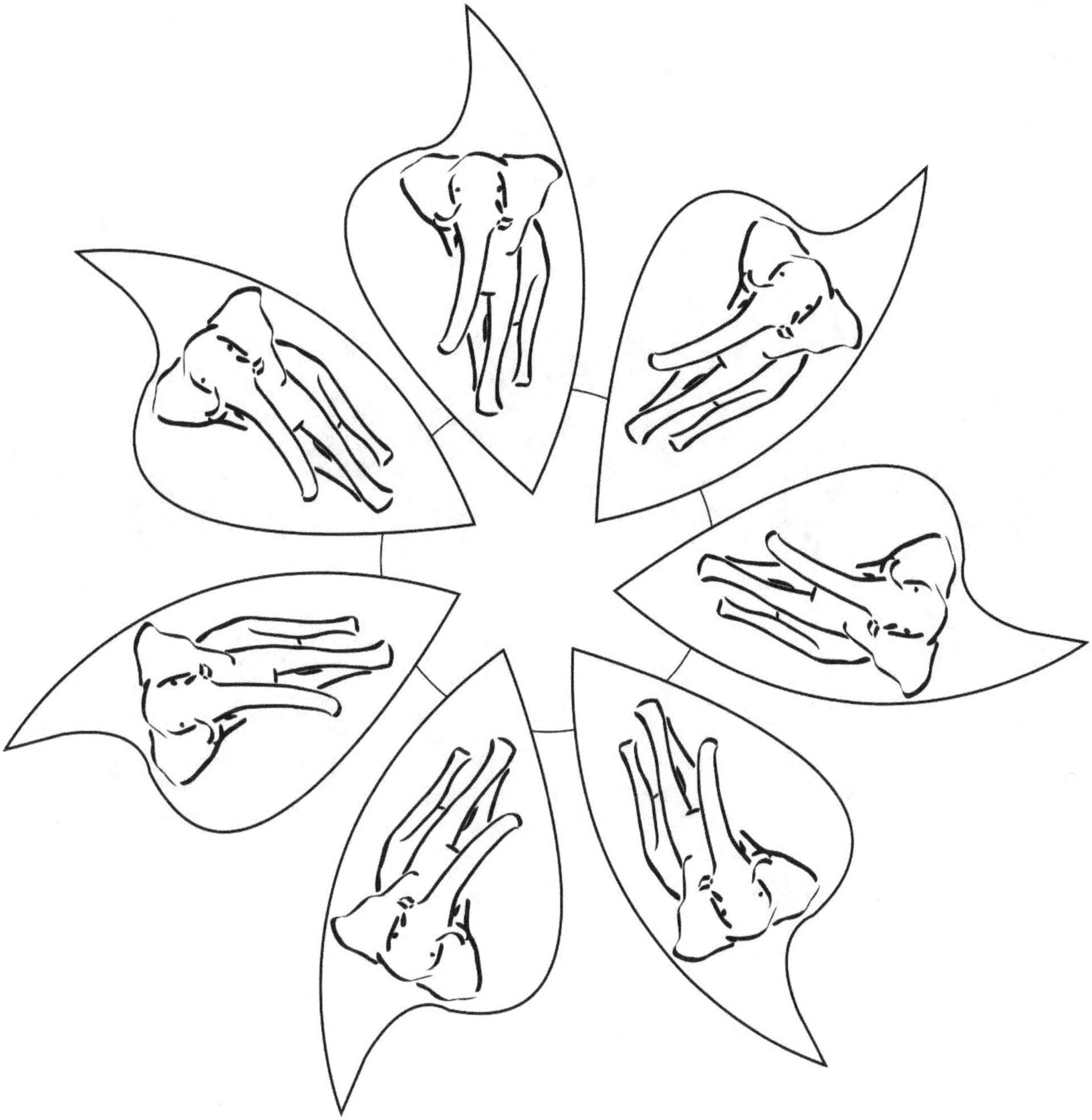

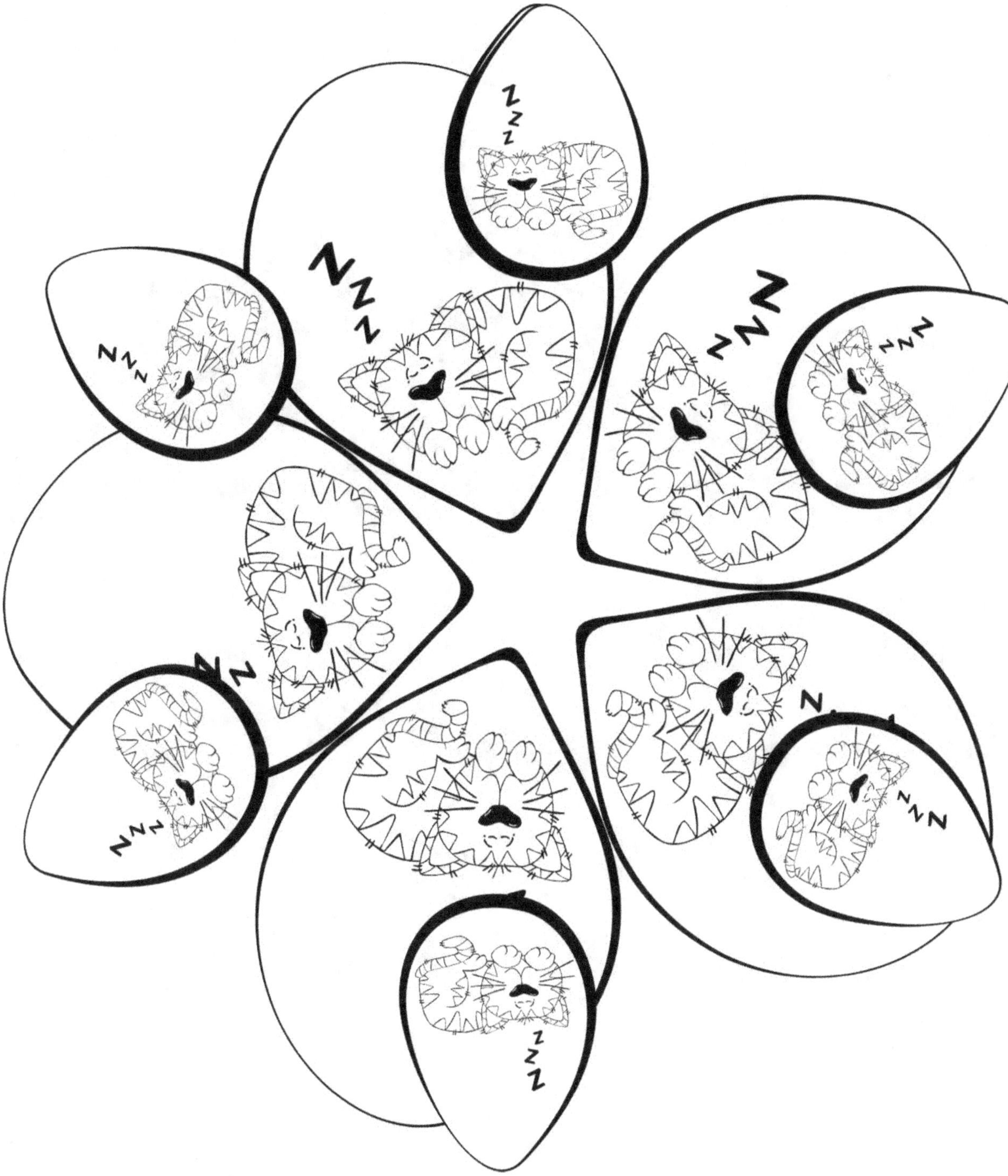

www.ingramcontent.com/pod-product-compliance
Lightning Source LLC
Chambersburg PA
CBHW080817180526
45168CB00006B/2482
* 9 7 8 1 5 1 8 6 4 8 2 3 6 *